Druidry
and Meditation

Exploring how meditation can
enhance your Druidic practice

Druidry
and Meditation

Exploring how meditation can
enhance your Druidic practice

Nimue Brown

MOON
BOOKS

Winchester, UK
Washington, USA

First published by Moon Books, 2012
Moon Books is an imprint of John Hunt Publishing Ltd., Laurel House, Station Approach,
Alresford, Hants, SO24 9JH, UK
office1@o-books.net
www.o-books.com

For distributor details and how to order please visit the 'Ordering' section on our website.

Text copyright: Nimue Brown 2011

ISBN: 978 1 78099 028 6

A CIP catalogue record for this book is available from the British Library.

Design: Stuart Davies

Printed and bound by CPI Group (UK) Ltd, Croydon, CR0 4YY
Printed in the USA by Offset Paperback Mfrs, Inc

We operate a distinctive and ethical publishing philosophy in all
areas of our business, from our global network of authors to
production and worldwide distribution.

CONTENTS

While this is a book aimed primarily at Pagans and Druids, it should be accessible to anyone wishing to explore different aspects of solitary and group meditation. This is not a book that will teach you everything you need to know about how to be a Druid, but it might set you off in some useful and interesting directions. This is a broad introduction to meditation, suitable for total beginners but also intended to be useful to more experienced folk who wish to journey deeper.

Introduction

When I first came to Druidry, there weren't a great many texts to be had explaining how to be a Druid. I read what I could find, and while that gave me broad brushstrokes, I wanted a much more precise guide on how to go about doing 'it'. I wanted someone to tell me what to do. What does it mean to be a Druid? How do you live as a Druid? I wasn't only interested in ritual practice, but in the detail of ordinary life, in Druidry as integral to every day existence. Over the years, studying with OBOD, attending talks and workshops, lurking about on forums and listening to others, I picked up a great many different and not always compatible ideas about what Druidry is and means. Once I started participating in rituals, I learned by doing and observing. On occasion, people tried to tell me what to do and I found myself irritated by them. I learned that I did not want to be told exactly how to go about being a Druid after all.

I have lost track of how many times someone has written, or said in my presence that Druidry cannot be found in books. It has to be experienced. Which makes the idea of writing a useful book about Druidry seem like a bit of a nonsense. But in much the same way, a book cannot make you a kitchen cupboard either. It can tell you about tools, materials, potential problems and show you pictures of other people's cupboards to inspire you. Making the cupboard remains your responsibility.

So where do you go to experience it? Where does the path begin?

I learned, in frustration, that Druidry isn't really a thing one person can teach another, because it is unique to each of us. But that still doesn't answer the question of where to start and how to search for it. Then some years ago, I started acquiring people who wanted to learn, and who thought I had something to teach them. That was a surprising process, but sharing what I know has taught me a great deal. No, you can't teach Druidry and you can't put it in a book. Anyone who wants to be a Druid, must, in the end, find their own way, that's part of the nature of the thing. What you can do is put tools in people's hands and tell them how to use them, much like the cupboard making metaphor. You can share techniques for exploring, and stories of how you found your own path. You can wave to other folk when you see them roaming along some other route through the great forest that is Druidry. I can pass onto you the things I've picked up, as you will no doubt pass along anything that seems useful or relevant. We can't turn each other into Druids, but we can share around maps and tales from the road.

Therefore, this is another book that won't teach you how to be a Druid. But hopefully it won't be teaching you, in ways you'll find helpful and productive as you figure things out for yourself.

Chapter One

What is Meditation?

The commonly held image of meditation is of clearing the mind to a state of calm blankness. This is the meditation accompanying spiritualities that seek to transcend the flesh and mortal life. Clearing the mind is a useful trick to master. However, meditation is a far more diverse tool that can be used in all manner of ways and for a variety of purposes. Creating calm is a necessary part of meditation, but not the entirety of its scope. Meditating can just as easily be an exercise in focus and deep connection as an emptying of the mind. Focused, thoughtful meditation is, in my experience, a lot more interesting than seeking freedom from thought, and is frequently a lot more productive. It opens the mind to free flowing creativity, enabling us to find solutions and inspiration.

Druidry is not a religion that seeks to transcend physical experience. Our spirituality is rooted in nature and nourished by experience. We seek connection, relationship and inspiration, and the carefully emptied mind does not nurture any of these things.

This book is not about meditation that transcends the body. Druidry embraces physicality and honors our tangible selves. We are not meditating to escape from the material aspect of our being. Some exercises will take us deeper into physical awareness, strengthening our relationships with our own bodies, rather than seeking to deny them or transcend them. We are physical beings, and exploring the spiritual does not mean we have to somehow overcome our bodies. Our flesh connects us to nature and the material world, it is the basis from which we form relationships and experience life. Druidic meditation is entirely rooted in the body, and can be intensely involved with the real world around us.

The classic image of seated composure for meditation is also something we can cast aside from the outset. There are a great many ways of meditating, some decidedly active and sound laden! Meditating need not be a solitary activity either, and group work confers many benefits. Good meditation takes us deeper into awareness, life and our own being, rather than removing us from any of these precious things.

Through this book, I'll set out different forms of meditation, focusing on different aspects of living. There will be a mix of broad principles and specific examples, as well as outlines for creating your own workings specific to your personal needs, circumstances and beliefs.

At its most basic level, meditation is a tool for relaxation. In this capacity, it is good for relieving stress and anxiety, easing tension from the body and clearing the mind of the turmoil of daily troubles. By creating pools of inner calm, we can better deal with the challenges of living. By physically relaxing, we can reduce the amounts of pain we experience, improve overall health, enable sleep and enhance quality of life. Improved awareness of our own bodies allows us to better work with and within ourselves.

Meditation can also be used as mental exercise, providing a workout for the imagination. Our minds are no different from our bodies, and deprived of playful activity, imaginations wither as surely as muscles do. Taking the time to meditate in creative ways is a means of engaging our creative potential, opening ourselves to inspiration and getting in the habit of thinking in wilder, more exciting ways. The experience of playful imagination meditating can bring, is a great enabler and nourishes creativity. We can use meditation for problem solving, tackling psychological issues and exploring the landscapes of our own minds.

By becoming intently aware of and focused on things other than ourselves, we can deepen our consciousness of them and further our understanding. For anyone following a Druidic path, this form of working is inherently spiritual. We seek a closer relationship with the natural world, which we can develop by being more fully aware of it. We can actively seek spiritual experience through meditation and use the tools of meditation to increase spiritual awareness in everyday life.

The calm, quiet spaces enabled by meditation open us to forms of listening not so immediately available at other times. In ritual, making the call for peace, the lines 'for without peace, the voice of spirit cannot be heard' are frequently included. When our minds are awash with noise and chaos, we cannot hear the voice of our own spirit, much less anything beyond us. Developing a spiritual awareness takes time and quiet. Meditation is a discipline that creates the possibility for this.

Druidry as a religion is very much about individual responsibility and experience. No amount of reading or listening to others can substitute for the insight that comes from doing. There are numerous ways of exploring a Druidic path, meditation is just one approach amongst many, but it does enable and support other ways of experiencing to good effect. The exercises that take us closer to nature nourish our Druidry. Creativity is prized within Druidry, so the scope for meditation to bring inspiration is a very useful one. Visualization can be used in magical practice, pathworkings can be used in ritual, and meditation leads the way to Shamanic journeying, for people called in that direction. The mental discipline that comes from meditating, and the capacity for self-control and finding calm, are all useful skills that enrich Druidry and enable us to bring Druidry into our daily lives.

This book explores personal meditation practice and the running of group sessions as well as looking at how to use meditation in ritual settings. I have been meditating for the entirety of my adult life, have run meditation sessions for pagan and non-pagan groups, and have worked with meditation in ritual. I've also had the opportunity to attend meditation sessions run by skilled practitioners from different pagan and spiritual backgrounds.

While I am glad to share what I have learned in the last decade or so, solitary meditation is just that – working alone means holding sole responsibility for your wellbeing. Running a meditation group means taking responsibility, to a degree, for those who work with you. Meditation is not without risk. It can take us into uncharted regions of the self, opening up old wounds and bringing difficult, painful things into the light. It might have a fuzzy New Age image, but meditation is not an entirely safe activity and needs treating with respect. It is not a self-indulgent toy to be dabbled with thoughtlessly. Handled carelessly it can bring problems – as can anything. Yet at the same time approaching meditation with an open heart and a playful spirit is often the best way forward. Meditation should be undertaken mindfully, which does not preclude enjoying it and having fun, but does require a responsible attitude.

The most important thing to remember is this: You are in control. When you meditate, you always have the option of opening your eyes, pulling back from the experience and drawing breath. What you imagine, or see, is yours. If you do not like what you find on your journeying, that's something you will have to deal with, but it remains yours, and can be handled. That which lurks in the shadows of our psyches is fearful in part because we cannot see it. The process of drawing these things out into view may be uneasy, but it is also liberating. Anything we encounter within ourselves is part of us and part of an experience we have full control over. So long as we hold awareness of our own power and ability to choose, we will not be swamped by any meditation experience.

Dealing with fears, wounds and ghosts through meditation can be a lot more manageable than trying to tackle them head-on in everyday life. It can also be sudden and immediate, with aspects of self and history coming to the surface in unexpected ways. Plunging into memory and identity, we might well find buried nightmares. But we can and will also find a clearer sense of self, the core of our strength and the means to move forwards. For every buried skeleton, there will also be treasures. Self-knowledge is a precious thing to have. Insight and understanding serve us well in every aspect of living. Knowing that we are self-possessed and in control of our feelings and experiences is enabling. If we do not know ourselves, our scope for living is sorely limited. Once we know, we are able to act, to change, to take control. The more thoroughly we understand anything, the better equipped we are to manage it, find the good in it, and find our own happiness.

Loosely speaking, the goal of any spiritual path is radical self-improvement – through enlightenment, transcendence, revelation, merging with deity, becoming one with the universe, or however else you choose to conceptualize it. We wish to become more than we are. We have the capacity within us to be more than we are, but the journey that is about self must begin with self, and with self-knowledge.

When to Meditate

The choice of timing for meditation depends a lot on what you wish to achieve. Some people find it helps to set apart a specific amount of time for meditation each day, others prefer to slot it in at need or on a whim. There is no right answer here. There is no necessity to meditate at a certain frequency. Meditating for the sake of it confers no real advantages. We are not clocking in hours; we will not be scored on effort or rewarded for time invested. It is only the quality of the experience that matters. And so, being a Druid does not mean daily meditation, or spending an hour each week in a certain place, or posture. It is a matter of finding a way of working that makes sense and suits your needs and purposes. Below are some examples of possible meditation times and their specific usefulness.

Meditating first thing in the morning, perhaps even from the comfort of your bed, makes it possible to greet the day slowly and move into it from a state of calm. Life may sometimes necessitate leaping up in response to an alarm clock, but there's a lot to be said for letting yourself wake naturally when possible. Taking the time to gather thoughts and contemplate the day ahead makes it easier to step out into the world in a state of preparedness. If time is short, stopping for a few deep breaths and a brief calming and centering exercise can make a great deal of difference to how you experience the day. Scrambling around in a state of panic isn't a productive way of being. Meeting the day's chaos and trials from a state of equilibrium is far more effective.

This probably isn't the time for long, convoluted pathworkings or anything deeply intellectual in nature. It is a good time to explore the content of dreams, gently meandering the borderlands between sleep and waking. It is a good time to stretch, exploring physical presence, feeling your body respond to the day. It might be useful to take the time to greet the sun, meditate on the view from the window, or enliven yourself with a chant, or by repeating affirmations, prayers or other things you find helpful.

Taking time to meditate first thing – be it only a few minutes, is a way of asserting yourself, and your ownership of the day. You can find a few minutes for you, the rest of life can spare you that much. You do not have to hit the ground running. Letting go of the sense of pressure and urgency, taking the time for self, we might instead hit the ground dancing, walking and skipping, more centered within ourselves and more conscious as we set forth.

Taking time to meditate during the day can create oases of peace and respite. It isn't necessary to devote great swathes of time to meditation – under pressure, a few moments taken to still body and mind, and mentally regroup can be very helpful. Again, this is an assertion of self, a claiming back from the hubbub that fills too many people's lives. In times of stress, stepping back and demanding a few moments to think rather than being forced to react, can make all the difference between a good call and a bad one. In slowing down, we serve ourselves well. Equally, in times when we lack focus and direction or are struggling to find energy, brief periods spent meditating can help resolve these issues. It is an assertion of self and self-control and can be brought to bear in any circumstance.

Certain kinds of meditations – especially pathworkings with narrative threads, require longer stretches of time and guaranteed tranquility. They cannot be squeezed into moments stolen from a hectic day. Nor is it feasible to step in and out of them in response to external pressures. They need planning for and demand commitment. To undertake a more involved meditation, or work in deep contemplation with a place or entity, requires the dedication of time. It's also best to do this kind of work when you are wakeful and able to concentrate properly on it. Therefore, involved meditation needs to be a daytime activity. You might choose to do it in an evening after work or set aside weekend time. It is fine to meditate without taking on these more involved workings if they do not suit your circumstances.

Even in the most chaotic family home or shared house, it is often possible to find quiet places for evening meditation. Gardens, porches and other outside spaces may help. I find bathrooms are frequently a good option – the lockable door and the scope to get under a shower or into a soothing bath is conducive to meditation. If there is a great deal of noise and disturbance, it may be necessary to ask for an hour of quiet once in a while. This is worth exploring for its own sake – the urge towards noise, especially background noise, and rowdiness might be 'normal' but that doesn't make it good for us. Having peaceful time within your own home is beneficial.

One of the advantages of group meditation is that a shared commitment to meeting and meditating makes it easier to stick to. If time is in short supply, solitary meditating can be harder to maintain. Gathering socially to meditate, in a space that has been agreed upon for that use creates boundaries both in time and environment. Those around us may 'forget' that we asked for quiet when we meditate alone, but it's difficult to miss a room full of people all being quiet. The additional social aspect of group meditation is an added bonus, and the process of sharing affirms the experience. Shared meditation is a lovely evening activity.

Meditation on the brink of sleep can enhance your scope for resting. For anyone who suffers insomnia, it can be a way of tackling sleeplessness, or at least helping the body to rest to some degree. If you have trouble letting go of waking concerns to move into a restful state, meditation can help with this process. Techniques for relaxing the body are especially useful in facilitating sleep. This is not a time to try anything too complex or emotionally demanding, but it works well to use simple, familiar exercises. As being in bed means lying down in a warm, relaxed and darkened place, with no pressure to be anywhere else imminently, it's an ideal space to work with.

I have heard some people express the feeling that meditation before sleep is not a good idea because your concentration is impaired. There is also the issue of becoming too involved in the meditation to settle properly – which is largely a matter of picking appropriate techniques in the first place. Others feel that meditation before sleep makes lucid dreaming more likely, or even that you may be able to shape the dreams that follow it. For example if you meditate upon a question, your dreams may offer an answer to it. Working around sleep it is important not to dwell on things that upset or disturb you, as these will keep you awake – which serves no purpose. Be disciplined about the concepts you work with. I assume that some people will find pre-sleep meditation more likely to keep them awake, and that others will not. As this is bound to be a very individual issue, you will have to ascertain whether or not it suits you and proceed accordingly.

Meditation is not separate from life, and can be woven into daily living in all kinds of ways. Once you develop the habit of pausing, breathing, contemplating and becoming calm, it's possible to do that in almost any place or situation; thus meditating moves a person into more aware ways of living and being. In this aspect, it very much supports your Druidry.

What Kit do you Need?

New Age shops will happily sell you any amount of kit to aid you in your meditation – incense to burn, soothing background music, whale sounds, mats to sit upon, clothing to wear ... . You can spend as much money as you want to, but none of it is strictly speaking necessary.

Kit is not without its uses however. If you find it difficult to create a conducive atmosphere or to step away from your normal activities, designating space, items or gear as part of your practice may be helpful. If calming your mind and relaxing your body are difficult, then soothing aids, such as mellow music and soft lighting may assist. Sometimes it helps to have specific routines to reinforce the shifting of states, or assist in making the right atmosphere. If these help to you, then by all means use them.

It is important to recognize that anything you use alongside meditation is an aid, not an integral part of the process. All you need to meditate is the determination to do so. It is possible to meditate in any space, with background noise, disturbance and distractions, if the will is there. We do not need to be separate from our environment to meditate, nor do we necessarily need tranquility – although whilst learning techniques, peace is a distinct advantage! However, the peace and control we seek lie within us and have nothing to do with our external environments.

Too much dependence on supportive 'gear' can become a disadvantage. If we need the right lighting, ambient music and incense to find our meditate state, then we are limited to meditating only in that pre-organized circumstance. A dependence on the right clothes, the right colored candle and so forth takes power away from us. We risk ascribing what we do to our props, not our own efforts. We also deny ourselves the useful tool that is meditation in self-defense.

Once you are confident about a meditation, you may find you can use it in times of stress and challenge. Visualizations, calming techniques, and so forth can be tremendously useful utilized in times of pressure and need. Crises do not wait for the whale CD to go on, and are no respecter of whether we happen to be wearing the right gear. To use meditation to its fullest effect, it's important to feel confident doing it in any conditions, and therefore worth avoiding any feeling of dependence on external things.

It is also worth noting that music, incense and mood lighting belong entirely to the realm of stationary indoors meditation, and that's not the only way to meditate. Working outdoors, or in public spaces, we won't have access to these things. While the early sections on this book are wholly related to living room practice supported by conducive gear, later sections are not.

Using mood-creating tools also acts to insulate us from the world. This is an issue to approach carefully. Peace is desirable, and tranquility in our homes beneficial, but tuning out the actual sounds and smells around us in preference for ones we have selected, is not without issue. Meditation can be used to distance us from our surroundings and 'normal' life, in times of need, but this is not its only function. In Druidry we seek relationship, and that does not mean seeking the esoteric at the expense of the immediate. The place we are in, the way it sounds, smells and feels are important too, and there is much to be said for not blocking them out.

All of this said, it is important to be physically comfortable when meditating. It's hard to relax if your jeans are pinching or you are feeling cold. The gear you most critically need for meditating is whatever enables you to comfortably occupy the space you mean to use. For a short meditation, this is less of an issue, but if you intend to spend half an hour on a pathworking, you need to be physically comfortable for the duration. When working outside it is important to consider the vagaries of climate, and to make sure (unless you plan to stand) that you have something suitable under you. Damp ground does not do the body any good, nor does it aid concentration. We are not in the business of trying to negate or ignore physical experience, so making sure that bodily experience does not distract from intention is important. Physical comfort plays a big part in that. Meditation should be enjoyable, it should not involve unnec-essary suffering just to hold a pose, or stay in an unsuitable location.

When you are planning to meditate, choose clothing that suits the environment and temperature, and that allows you to move and sit comfortably. Pick attire that requires no attention from you. Make sure that technology cannot intrude on what you are doing – where possible, leave it behind, or at the very least, switch it off and put it out of sight. Being mindfully present will make you more aware of the humming of fridges, lights and other electrical items indoors. You may find this a distraction you want to be rid of. You may also become more aware of ambient light – standby buttons glowing in competition with your candles, light pollution from streetlights – these may affect your choice of when and where to work. You don't have to be stoical and tune things out – you can change your environment to suit you, or seek another place to work in. This is a process of learning about your own awareness and surroundings, so if you find things irritate you or impede meditation, explore that.

For stationary meditations, you will need a place that is physically comfortable – working inside you have beds, sofas, comfy chairs, floor cushions, the bathtub, a pillow on the floor and all manner of other options to explore. Play with these, and see what feels right. Different arrangements suit different moods and times of the day. Changing the place you meditate in can significantly alter the experience. Again, there are no right or wrong answers here, only scope for experience and finding what suits you. Working outdoors, you have weather and ground conditions to contend with – so meditation gear could well be wellington boots and a waterproof coat. The key thing is that it must work for you.

Chapter Two

Meditation for the Body

The mind and body are not separate things. Each influences the other, for good and for ill. However, this is something we can take control of to a significant degree. Taking care of our bodies enables us to think more clearly. Reducing mental stress improves bodily health. Meditation is a tool that helps with this process. For best effect, it needs to be supported with good eating, sleeping and exercise patterns. Meditation alone is not enough to create mental and physical wellbeing, but it can significantly contribute to the process. Being more aware of the state of both mind and body, we become more able to act for our own good. If we are continually rushing and pushing, it is harder to notice aches and pains, to recognize tiredness or a need to let off steam. Slowing down enables us to think about ourselves in different ways. Taking the time to pay attention, we become aware of our needs.

Until the body is able to maintain prolonged bouts of being both still and calm, it's very difficult to manage long meditations. The ability to remain motionless, not fidgeting or uncomfortable, takes a while to master. While we struggle with that, focusing on complex meditations is difficult. In meditating for the body and in ways that focus upon our physical selves, we make peace with ourselves. These meditations develop skills that enable more complex workings, but they are also useful in their own right. Self-awareness begins in the body – if we are not familiar with our own corporeal presences, then we are not going to know our own minds either.

Much of modern life discourages bodily awareness. We dress to hide our flesh, eat at set times not in response to hunger, wake for alarms and not from being sated. Most of us do not get much physical exercise; we take medicines that suppress our symptoms, use perfumes to mask our natural scents. We are in essence, animals. We are mammals, as fleshy, messy and vitally alive as every other mammal out there. And yet we deny this part of ourselves, and we learn to tune it out in order to conform to social pressure and the perceived demands of modern living. As Druids, we honor nature, and so we must also honor nature within ourselves. Exploring our own bodies and physicality, embracing our animal selves, honoring the elements within us and learning to relate to ourselves as physical beings is very much part of developing our Druidry.

Meditations that focus on the body are the easiest to learn and the best place to begin. They give us roots and solidity, enabling peacefulness. These are forms of meditation that can be used quickly and for short periods – meditations that might be used at need in self-defense when life throws hard things our way. Incorporated into daily life, they aid relaxation and self-awareness. The skills in this section create meditative states, which can then be developed in more complex visualizations and pathworkings. However, we do not transcend into higher levels when we work for the mind or the spirit. There may be increasing complexity, but that does not mean elevation or progress. To meditate deeply through focusing on your body can be just as profound as the most intellectually challenging of pathworkings. Perhaps more so. As the Zen proverb goes: 'Before Enlightenment, chop wood carry water, after Enlightenment, chop wood carry water.'

Breathing
Deep breathing has an instant, calming effect on the body. When we panic or go into fight/flight responses, accelerated heartbeat

and breathing are very much part of the process. Taking conscious control of your breathing and slowing it down will reduce the effects of panic and stress. We breathe deeply as we move into sleep, and slow, full breaths are very much part of our relaxation process. Much of the time, most people take quicker, shallower breaths than they could. Using our lungs to a greater degree is good for us.

Breathing deeply we become conscious of the most essential aspect of our physical selves. Breath is life. We cannot do without it for more than a few minutes. Breathing is a constant activity, yet we pay little attention to it. With deeper breathes, we can overcome anxiety and improve self-control.

Breathing techniques are barely discernable to others. They can be used in any time or place without drawing attention. A few moments of consciously controlled breathing can make a lot of difference.

Begin simply by being aware of your breath. Are you breathing with your ribcage, or is your stomach involved in the process too? How deeply do you normally breathe, and how rapidly? Slow down gently, deepen breaths and let your shoulders loosen. If you are tense, you might not be using your diaphragm properly. Take the time to relax and breathe deeply, letting your stomach move in and out as you do. Slow your breathing and fill your lungs generously each time. Don't force it or hold it in any uncomfortable way, but relax into it, and let your body loosen around the process of taking in and exhaling breath.

Being still and breathing slowly can quieten the mind and body without any further conscious effort being needed. Sometimes it is enough just to do this. You may wish to explore how different positions affect your breathing – sitting, standing, lying down, eyes open, eyes closed. You may also wish to experiment with holding between breaths – after the inhale, the exhale or both. I find it beneficial to do this consciously when first slowing my breathing, and then to let my body settle into its own rhythm. Avoid anything that causes discomfort – the point is to relax, not to push yourself towards any kind of feat of breath holding or control.

As you breathe, you can become more conscious of the air drawn into your body. Think about the temperature of it, and any smells you are aware of. Is it damp air, or dry? And what about the out breath? What do you perceive of yourself in breathing out? What does your body do when you breathe slowly and deliberately? You may become conscious of tension – shoulders and stomach are most common, but other places may make their discomfort known to you. If you need to move, stretch or loosen off, then do so, and then relax again. The process of relaxing can also cause other natural body reactions, like flatulence. Take this as a good sign, it means your digestive system isn't tense! Relaxing is often a cyclical process. After stopping, aches and pains become more apparent. Addressing them allows further relaxation, during which other issues may come to the surface. Emotional tensions may also become apparent, and these too we must deal with to enable peacefulness.

Breathing Exercises

Here are some simple meditations to combine with your conscious deep breathing.

1) When you breathe in, be conscious of the air entering your body – think of it as sky and space, wind, and the breath drawn by every other living thing. Let your thoughts run freely through everything you associate with air, all that it means to you. Be aware of the life and vitality the air brings you and your relationship with it as you take air in and breathe it out.

2) As you breathe in, think of some positive energy or quality you wish to take into yourself. That might be calmness, energy, patience or something else entirely. Every time you breathe in, repeat that thought to yourself. You might just want to use the focus word, contemplate the emotional state you are breathing, or think a specific intention.

3) You can develop the previous exercise by picking a corresponding negative thing to breathe out. Therefore, if you are breathing in calmness, you could then breathe out tension, repeating the concept with every breath and trying to engage physically with the process.

4) You can also pair your in breath positivity with a giving back. If you breathe in community, you might breathe out friendship. Breathing in inspiration you might then breath out the intention to let that flow into the world.

5) To take the above exercise further, you do not have to limit yourself to one inhale and one exhale concept. You can move from one idea to the next as the inspiration takes you – so long as this remains a calm and fluid activity. If looking for things to breathe in or out becomes self competitive or stressful, you are defeating the object, and if it sends your brain haring in mad and random directions you may wish to return to a simpler version. Otherwise, flow with the natural associations and see what comes to you.

6) You can make the breathing exercise into more of a visualization if that appeals to you. As you breathe in you can visualize the air entering your lungs and moving out around your body through your blood. Breathe out with

the image of carbon dioxide leaving your body. You may also visualize this as energy, you might see air energy as white, or blue and want to envisage that filling you as you breathe in, and define that which you breathe out with a different color. If working at night, you may be breathing in darkness rather than light. If you are working with breathing in positive energy and breathing negativity out, you may wish to color that with visualizations. For example, you may be breathing in the rich greens of the woodland around you and breathing out the grey smoke of your workplace. You may be breathing in calming shades of blue and breathing out some kind of orange paisley expression of frustration.

Untensing

The process of consciously breathing can flag up tension. Being tense inhibits movement and causes pain, and far too many people suffer from it. Human bodies were designed for the kinds of stresses that can be dealt with by flight or fight reactions. The world we have created for ourselves, full of psychological pressures and situations where it's not ok to just hit the problem over the head, or run away from it, means a lot of us spend our days getting tense. Once you start paying proper attention to your body, any such tensions become a lot more apparent. There are other issues that can cause bodily pain – poor posture, an insufficiently supportive mattress, an out of date glasses prescription, as well as medical conditions. If you experience pain that does not respond to relaxation techniques, you might want to seek medical advice.

Exercise is the best way of relieving stress and thus reducing tension. It gives your body chance to do something like a natural response. You might not be able to run away from your boss or customers, but running after hours will go a long way towards making you feeling better. Any kind of sport or bodily activity will benefit you in this regard. Meditation alone is not enough to deal with pent up frustration and stress, but it can help.

When you undertake a conscious breathing exercise, you may become aware of pain or tension in your body. The first thing to do is seek physical solutions – stretching and flexing may relieve the tension. A change of position may also help. Break with the breathing mediation and see what you can do to become more comfortable. Once you are at ease, begin again with the breathing. As you untense one part of your body, you may become more conscious of discomfort in other areas, so this is a process that can take a while to complete. Even if you can't untense everything, any progress you make will be a benefit.

Untensing Exercises

You can encourage your muscles to relax just by concentrating on doing so. This takes time and a little practice. We have far more scope for conscious control of our bodies than is always apparent. If the tension is merely caused by stress, then mental determination to release it is enough to reverse the process.

1) Focus on the part of your body most in need of attention. Flex and stretch that area as much as circumstances permit. Spend a while focusing on slow deep breathing to settle yourself, and then concentrate your attention on the afflicted area. With each out breath, try to relax the muscles. If you are dealing with a complex part of yourself – like a hand, you might want to concentrate on one small area at a time – like a finger, working through until you have relaxed the whole. You may need to flex and stretch repeatedly as you go.

2) If you are seeking general relaxation and untensing, you

can apply the above exercise to your entire body. I find it helps to start either at the head or the toes and work towards the other end, trying to be methodical about direction. Deliberate focus on untensing muscles will result in them relaxing – this is an exercise that gets easier and more effective with repetition. The first few times through it is challenging. Just trying to figure out where your muscles are and what any pain relates to can take time if you are not in the habit of paying attention to yourself. If you stick with it, you will make progress.

3) As an alternative to mentally relaxing your body by willing it so, you may find it works better to imagine something happening to you that would cause you to relax – such as being massaged, or floating in warm water. Imagining warmth spreading through your body can aid relaxation as well.

4) You can combine this relaxation strategy with the breathing exercise – breathing out tension and breathing in calm, envisaging soothing warmth permeating your body with each breath.

Opening Joints Exercise

When I was studying Tai Chi some years ago, the teacher introduced us to the idea of opening joints through meditation. The free flow of energy through the body is a key concept in Tai Chi and the philosophy around it. Anything that blocks the flow of energy is bad for us – acupuncture works with the same theory, opening blockages. I remember him saying that if you could open your joints out such that you became an inch taller, legend had it that you would live forever.

Whether or not there is any literal truth in this, working with awareness of your joints makes for a good meditation exercise. It's a way of thinking that adds to your self-awareness, aids relaxation, and creates some interesting mental challenges. This is a good follow-up meditation once you have untensed your body.

Envisage a small ball of golden light between each of your joints. This is actually a lot harder than it first sounds, once you start considering hands, feet and spine. There are many bones in the human body. If you are not predisposed to thinking visually, this can be a very difficult idea to hold in your head on one go, and you might prefer to work on one area at a time. Again, this is an exercise that gets easier with repetition.

Once you have the balls of light mentally in place, imagine them stretching and growing, opening the joint out gently, and with warmth so that energy can flow around your body more easily. It's a very relaxing exercise regardless of whether you are able to affect your height or longevity.

Self-Awareness
Once you are completely relaxed, you may wish to use meditation time to increase your self-awareness. It's amazing how oblivious to our own bodies and feelings we can become. Taking the time to be present in our own skins, listening to ourselves and exploring how we feel, is a journey in its own right.

When you are still and calm, relaxed and breathing deeply, you can become more aware of the rest of your body. How do your feet feel? Are you hungry? Thirsty? What temperature is your body at? Does your skin feel comfortable, or too dry? How fast is your heart beating? How heavy do you feel? This is time in which you can get to know yourself as a physical entity, exploring where your edges lie, finding the shape of you. In terms of building your self-awareness this is important work.

Knowing yourself does not just mean knowing your mind.

Self-Awareness Exercises

1) Try and fully feel your body in its entirety, filling your awareness with consciousness of your physical being.

2) Visualize your body as though you were looking at it from the outside. Try and picture yourself from different angles.

3) Visualize your body filling with light – think carefully about where the edges of you are. Explore both seeing and feeling this light-filled you.

4) Visualize your body filling with darkness in just the same way as you have with light. Explore the differences.

5) You can develop this visualization in any way that appeals to you – water, fire, air, wood, leaves, forms of energy, soil etc. When you are exploring later meditations to do with connection and empathy, you might want to return to this exercise and re-explore it.

Calming and Focusing Exercises

There's nothing like stress or emotional turmoil for making it hard to concentrate, and of course it's the times of stress and emotional turmoil when we most need to have our wits about us. This calls for something I have long thought of as 'Druidry in self-defense' – tools at our disposal that we can use when we need them.

These are concepts it's fun to play with, and good imaginative workouts, so are worthwhile even if you don't think you need them defensively. However, with them in place, we can draw on them at need. The more accustomed we are to holding a particular thought or idea, the easier it is to do so. Thus creating and developing thought forms during periods of calm and ease, we have them at our disposal when under pressure.

Firstly, take the time to consider what helps you feel safe and secure. Whatever it is, this is what you will work with. You might want to imagine your ancestors stood behind you, or a very big sword in your hands, for example. Anything that gives you courage and reminds you of yourself has potency. My personal favorite, used over many years, is the image of myself with huge, black scaly dragon wings. I can fold them around me when I feel defensive, or have them big and looming if I need to brazen my way through something.

In times of stress, conjuring up such images serves a number of purposes. They give us something else to think about, and that can be very helpful for distracting from panic. They remind us of the things that give us strength and courage, and they remind us of our Druidry. The act of calling up a visualization is inherently calming, and is a way of taking control of the self, and thence the situation. It's difficult to feel more than one thing at a time, so if you are encouraging yourself to feel something helpful you are less likely to be overwhelmed by a dysfunctional emotion.

A second option is to envisage yourself within a protective bubble. You can imagine that bubble being made of any substance that works for you, and surround yourself with it. Sunlight, steel, crystal, water, energy – there are many choices, and whatever works is good. Again, much of the power here comes from reminding yourself of your own rootedness and strength, and going through a mental process that will affirm your position and create calm so that you can better handle what is happening.

Another good exercise for gaining calm and focus is to concentrate on your center of gravity – which is probably in the region of your navel, and to visualize an egg, stone or crystal there – again go with the imagery that most suits you. Imagining the weight and solidity of the stone, deep inside you, giving you weight and substance, can be a good focus when you need to turn inwards for a little while and ground yourself.

It is worth practicing these when nothing else is going on; so that you know what tools will work for you and can call them to mind quickly. If you have the option, there is much to be said for taking calming and focusing exercises outside. Then, better still, you have your feet (or at least shoes) upon the earth. This literal grounding can be very powerful, and if you are able to change your environment, that can be highly beneficial too for breaking the situation and claiming the space to take control of it. Often the best thing to do with unpleasant situations is remove yourself from them. Even if it's only for a few minutes, stepping back helps you regain control. If you are obliged to remain however, hold in your mind the thought that the earth is, relatively speaking, not far beneath you. The distance from it is not so great when compared to the enormity of the earth itself. You are rooted, secure, and in holding confidence in your own ability to stay calm and cope, you are better equipped to get through.

If a thing is truly impossible or unbearable, then the only viable thing to do is acknowledge it and demand the space you need. Self-awareness means recognizing when you are beaten or set back, acknowledging your limitations and working within them, rather than persistently trying to push beyond breaking point. Stopping and stepping back can enable a second go, or facilitating seeing a way through where pushing and panicking do not serve at all.

Elemental Exercises

These are a series of meditations that work specifically with elemental imagery. Everything in the physical world can be connected to one or more the elements, so contemplating these ideas and connecting them with our own bodies helps us focus on our relationships with wider reality. Earth, Air, Fire and Water traditionally correspond with the four directions. Earth in the north, air in the east, fire in the south and water in the west is normal for Druidry although other traditions may use different correlations. This connection between direction and elements is used in ritual, so developing a deeper understanding of them enhances ritual practice. Connecting ritual Druidry with our self-awareness will inform what we do in ritual, and help bring that sense of ritual sacredness into the rest of our lives. In exploring the elements, we also explore our connections with all other living and non-living things, placing our sense of self within a web of connection and interdependence.

These are especially good meditations to use at the end of the day. They are gentle, affirming and it is easy to slip from them into sleep without leaving anything incomplete or creating strange dreams!

1) Once you have settled into a calm, meditative state, begin by thinking about your legs and feet. This is the part of your body that grounds you to the earth. Contemplate the strength that holds you up, the firmness that keeps you steady. Feel your connection to the ground, your rootedness. Be aware of your solidity. When you are ready, move your attention upwards to your stomach, and be conscious of the water that flows through your body. The streams, rivers, oceans and rain are inside you. Feel their presence in you and the way you flow with

them. Be aware of your dependence on water, how it is within you, and how you can be within it. Move up again to your lungs, and contemplate the presence of air within your body, the wind and sky drawn in when you breathe, bringing life, voice and freedom; the energy of air flowing into your blood, bringing life to your being. Feel the lightness of yourself, the air within you and the air against your skin. Then finally turn your attention to your head, and the fire of inspiration, energy and spirit burning within your mind. Feel the sun within you, the vibrancy of existence and the spark of your own awareness. Think how the sun nourishes and warms you, and how you in turn can share that energy and inspiration with others. You might like to try holding a consciousness of all four elements at the same time.

2)   You can extend and deepen the above exercise by taking each element in turn and exploring its correspondences within your body. For this, you may want to work one element at a time, but it does work to run all four together in an extended meditation session.

Earth: In many ways, our bodies belong to the earth. Our flesh is made of the same matter as other living things, and in death, we ultimately return to the soil. Our bones, the hard core of us, are made of calcium and connect us to the rocks. Our diets bring minerals into us that permeate our flesh and facilitate our existences. Salt especially is critical for life. The food we eat either had its roots in the soil, or fed on that which did. Plants belong to the earth, although they, like us, connect with all other elements too. In death, we return to the soil, the molecules of our being separating and becoming new forms. Meditating on the earth within us, we can also contemplate the many forms earth takes – mud, clay, soil and sand, mountain and desert, pebbles on the shore. Think about the textures of it, the weight and presence, the ways we encounter it externally in our lives. Envisage these different forms of earth pouring into you, feeding your bones, creating your strength. Feel the clay within you, contemplate that which comes from the earth and returns to it. Earth is centering, it is solidity, slow moving and reliable. The rich energy of soil nurtures life, and we depend upon it. Yet earth is also the wildness of earthquake and mudslide, the heat of lava and the drama of volcanoes. Earth is burial and decay, the breaking down of the past and the clay that reclaims us. Contemplate how you could improve your own relationship with earth, where you need more of it in your life, and where it requires more of you.

Water: Water permeates our beings, and without it, we cannot survive. We cannot go more than a few days without it. Our fluids are essential not only to our own lives, but to reproduction. Within us, water manifests as sweat, tears, semen, saliva, blood and digestive juices. We are made in water, and born in a rush of it. Our ancestors evolved within its embrace. Water is carried on our breath, emerging dramatically on winter days. We drink it, and it also nourishes everything we eat. Without water, there would be no plants, and no creatures for us to feed upon. Water is also cleansing, lifting the dirt from bodies and encouraging good health. It purifies us in a more spiritual sense as well. Water is the stuff of emotion and dream, its tides and currents touching our hearts. Pulled by the moon, it has powerful feminine connotations.

Water defines life on earth, and oceans cover the greater part of the earth's surface. Human civilization has depended on it, on streams, rivers, springs and wells for drinking and upon rivers and oceans for food and travel. We were able to make long journeys by boat long before land travel became easy for us. We look to the rain to keep crops alive and domesticated animals in good health. Water is also the mystery of mist and fog, the sky painting of clouds; it is grey relentless rain, the rising flood, the crash of wave and the tsunami. Think about the ways in which you encounter water, where it is joyful, or fearful, how it affects you. When do you seek it, or avoid it? What emotions does it inspire in you? Be aware of the liquid aspects of yourself. Do you drink enough? How do you feel about the fluids your body creates? Contemplate how you could improve your own relationship with water, where you need more of it in your life, and where it requires more of you.

Air: With every breath we draw, air enters our bodies, to be carried through to every cell. We can go mere minutes without it, before death ensues. Air is essential to the mind and it is our brains that die when air is denied us. It is also the voice within us, the gift of speech and song so essential in human culture. Air belongs to intellect and thought, to calm reason and careful logic. It is also freedom and possibility. It is the sky within us, and the whispers of the wind, the wild power of gales and the relief of a light breeze. It has driven windmills and sails, harnessed by human technology, and it carries all kinds of materials and messages as it travels. Continually touching our skin, air is the medium that bears sound to us. It touches us with wind, and the breath of others, tempts us with ideas of flight and the untamed skies. It is space and emptiness, the vast arc of the sky and the gentle breeze. It is also the tornado and hurricane, a battering from elements that care nothing for our wellbeing.

Feel the air within you. How does it taste? Where else has it been? What might be carried by it? What does freedom mean to you, and where would you go if you could ride the winds? When you speak, how does the air carry your voice, and what are you putting into it? Contemplate how you could improve your own relationship with the air, where you need more of it in your life, and where it requires more of you.

Fire: The spark of life, separating animate from inanimate, fire is every vital chemical reaction within us that allows our existence to continue from one moment to the next. Fire is the heat of combustion, the extraction of energy from food, the conversion of that energy into movement and potential. It is the tool our ancestors used, setting us apart from other creatures as we harnessed that most dangerous power for light, warmth and cooking. Fire is the hearth, the heart of the home, but it is also a weapon. It is the flame that turns raw materials into cheering foods, but it is equally the burning of heretics and witches. The blacksmith's fire makes ploughshares as readily as swords. Fire is potential and responsibility, it is the choice to turn something to creative, or destructive ends. We can make fireworks, or blow people up. It is the best, and the worst of all that we could be, and have been. Fire is also the heat of the sun, bringing light and life to all things. Without the sun, the plants would not grow and everything we eat carries some of that vital sun energy within it.

Feel the energy within you, and the sunlight you have ingested with your food. Be conscious of the energy around you, not just the sun on your skin, but the human- created energy around you, the fires we have harnessed to ease our lives. Consider your own use of those energies, how you feel about power, whether it alarms or excites you. Consider the things that inspire you to heat, in passion, rage or shame. Contemplate how you could improve your own relationship with fire, where you need more of it in your life, and where it requires more of you.

You might want to experiment with bringing the elements more literally into your meditations – standing in the rain or wind, kneeling with your hands upon the ground, holding a crystal, sitting beside a fire – there are many ways to increase your sense of connection and make the elements more immediate and obvious. Sitting with an element, you can contemplate it more directly, experiencing it as an external presence and feeling how it affects you. You can also consider how each of the elements manifests in the space you are using.

As you meditate on the elements, you may find other associations occur to you. Aspects of your personality may resonate with certain elements. You may feel parts of your life or experience tally with one element or another. In contemplation, you may find that one element features heavily in your life and sense of self, or that another is barely present for you. If this is so you may wish to seek greater balance, or you may decide that having one more profound elemental relationship suits you better. Elements are associated with birth signs, so you may wish to consider that in your meditations.

3) Each element contributes an essential quality without which life would not be possible. It is in the combining of all four elements that life exists. Contemplate the ways in which these elemental forces combine within you, as literal presences and as more esoteric ingredients of yourself.

4) Each element can impact upon us in beneficial or harmful ways. They can heal or destroy – we can cauterize or burn. They can cleanse us – the mud bath, smudging, water bathing, or letting the wind blow away the cobwebs. In destruction, all things return to the elements, and methods for letting go of the remains of the human dead all revolve around the elements, earth burial, burial at sea, exposure to the wind, or cremation. Consider the cycles of creation and destruction, healing and damage that the elements create, and consider where you are in relation to these.

Active Meditations

All of the previous set of meditations are very much about being still and turning the attention inwards. They are designed for situations where you sit or lie down. However, these are not the only ways of meditating. Where meditation is about relationship with our own bodies, it makes sense to consider using the body in more conscious ways rather than just leaving it lying around.

Any action can be undertaken in a meditative way. There is no need for the activity to be separate from regular life or 'special'. It is not the activity itself that makes for a meditation, but the way in which we approach it. Doing the dishes can be an act of meditation if we use it as a focus for meditative thinking. Tai Chi is considered to be a form of moving meditation, while Qi Gong is about standing meditations. Yoga uses poses to create meditative states. These are all traditions, which can be specifically learned. However, if there is no teacher to hand and no formal tradition available to study, a person can still experiment on their own. After all, every human tradition that exists does so because at some point, someone discovered or invented it. It isn't necessary to strike bizarre poses in order to meditate in a physical way, but you can if it suits you!

Active meditations create altered mental states through repetitive actions. You can explore them alone, but they also work well for situations of communal meditation. The list below isn't exhaustive, but covers some of the more obvious forms physical meditations can take. If something else speaks to you, explore it. There are no fixed ways of doing. Anything can be turned into a physical meditation – even housework if you have a mind to try it.

However, there is much to be said for exploring the more creative possibilities around physical meditations. The bardic aspect of Druidry prioritizes inspiration and creativity. Active, bodily meditations give us scope for beautiful creative expression. By moving slowly and with considered grace, we can turn any action into dance, and make poetry with the body. While any repeated action encourages trance, making that consciously beautiful gives other dimensions to the practice. It is not just a shifting of states; it is a gift to the self, and the world. Seeking beauty within meditation will predispose us to certain kinds of experience, and will also affect how we perceive ourselves as we are working.

Walking

The rhythm of walking has a soothing quality, good for body and mind alike. I find that very long walks put me in a meditative state without my even trying – anything over eight miles has some effect on me. Walking all day changes the pace of thought, slowing us to more natural tempos than the frantic rushing modern existence appears to demand. Walking puts feet in touch with the earth and opens us to experiencing landscape. We move closer to the sky, and potentially to the waters as well. If you fill that walking with noise, an iPod, or too much banter then you don't get chance to adjust into a different mindset. To make walking work as a meditation, first and foremost you must be present, aware of the walking and of the landscapes you pass through. A quiet acceptance of the journey and an easing into its slow speed is a meditation in itself.

Walking can also be used as a focus for more imaginative meditations. You can walk a pre-set path and use the shape of it to explore a concept – walking a circle to walk conceptually through the seasons of the year for example. You could plan a route that might reflect symbolically on your own life stages, allowing you to work through your own story. In the UK, there are many ancient ways, Roman roads and routes known to be older. If you can access such a route, you might choose to walk meditatively with the ancestors, contemplating their lives, values and wisdom. For those inclined to go further, there are old pilgrimage routes, and the ancient sites favored by modern pagans, all of which could be walked to, or around in a thoughtful way. You could undertake to walk for some days to a significant site, letting the journey become a spiritual act as you meditate your way through it. You might do that with a specific goal in mind, or simply for the experience.

Several years ago for a Peace One Day ritual, the Druid group I was with undertook to walk a fair few people into the woods and get them lost. Many of the people attending that ritual did not know the area, but there was a drummer at the point they needed to reach, and all of them eventually found their way. While they were walking, lost, and following the drums, we invited them to consider refugees in war zones, and what it must be like to walk with fear, not knowing which trees might hide a threat. It proved a powerful, affecting thing to do. In this way, walking can be combined with more imaginative meditations.

On other occasions, I've invited folks in rituals simply to walk out amongst the trees and spend some time being present, moving slowly through the landscape and being open to its voices. Walking out of the familiar space into darkness or a landscape we do not know begets experience, and handled meditatively, can become a journey inwards as well as over the terrain.

I spent several midsummers at British Camp in the Malverns, climbing the hill in darkness to wait for the dawn – another opportunity for walking meditation, where the journey becomes an act of ritual. Frequently, the boundaries between ritual, action and meditation grow hazy at such times. To me, that always feels like a sign that I'm getting it right, on some level.

To walk meditatively, begin by paying attention to your regular walking. How do you move? What does it feel like to connect your feet with the earth? Can you find the natural rhythm of your walking pace? How do your shoes affect you? You may find that you need better footwear – much modern attire, especially fashionable feminine footwear is not actually suitable for walking in. Feel the way your hops swing, and your arms move in time with your feet. Is your stomach involved in the process? How do you hold your head? Where are you looking, and what are you looking for?

Becoming aware of your body in motion, you will need to reinvestigate all of the things you contemplated whilst still. Find out who you are and how you move. Work on walking easily and with comfort, and on finding a pace you can maintain over longer distances. Pay attention to how long it takes to still your mind through walking even when you aren't meditating. Try walking whilst meditating upon your breathing. You might want to attach a concept to each footfall, or a phrase that can be repeated in time with your moving.

It is also interesting to experiment with slow walking. This can be undertaken indoors. See how slowly you can move, taking your body through the complex process each step involves. You will have to concentrate more on your balance than usual. Explore the shape or walking and the process of balance and unbalance it calls for.

Running

While walking meditations are fairly accessible, running requires levels of fitness and mobility not all of us have. Despite the practical similarities with walking, running affects body and mind in very different ways. The pace of it calls for a far more intense, moment to moment awareness of your body – especially if the terrain is challenging. Paying attention to the ground becomes critically important at the expense of perceiving wider surroundings. The force of feet hitting earth sends a regular drum beat of small shocks through the body, along with raised heartbeat, blood thundering in ears, and heavier breathing. We hear the sounds of our own bodies above all else when we run. Sweat inducing and rapidly exhausting, running pushes us into pain, and towards our own limits.

To run, or for that matter jog in a meditative way requires a commitment to physical fitness and stamina. The running will push you into a different headspace, but staying there long enough to do something meaningful is a lot harder. However, a runner can cover more distance than a walker, given the same time frames, and has an intense relationship with the ground they run upon. There is something wild and liberating about running – so many adults don't do it, after all. Breaking into a run when you aren't decked out like a jogger, but acting spontaneously for the joy of it, has a slightly subversive feel. If you cannot sustain longer running sessions, then the exuberance of a sudden, childlike dash through a less than perfectly suitable space, is good for the soul.

Being outdoor activities, walking and running should not be purely about fair weather and ease, if you can manage it. To be a Druid is to encounter nature in all its times and forms, from the cold shock of rain on an autumn night, to the clarity of a sharp morning. Having the right clothing and gear to be safe and responsible is important. Going wild, with no safety net has an allure, but if you get lost on a mountain, someone else will put themselves at risk to try to rescue you, more likely than not. To be a Druid is to be both wild, and responsible – and that's a fine balance to strike sometimes.

Dancing

When it comes to mixing beauty and contemplation in a single, physical act, dancing is the perfect form of expression. While dancing lends itself to social gatherings, it can also be a solitary act, and does not require an external source of music. You can dance to the music in your head, or to the strains of your own song. Any space with room enough to dance in is an option for dancing meditations – a woodland glade, a living room, or jumping like a crazy thing in a mosh pit. It's not the activity that defines the meditation, but the mindset.

You don't need much physical mobility to be able to dance –

slow movements are very expressive, and any capacity for movement at all will do. So, while we might associate dance with the grace, poise and athleticism of professionals, the reality is that most of us can dance. Dancing in a spiritual way, we have our relationship with the music to consider, if we use it, and our connection to the space we use. If the dancing is shared, then how we relate to others, physically, becomes part of the process too. We can dance to explore or express a concept or emotion. We can use it to stretch ourselves and explore the shapes our forms can create in the air. Dancing can be an expression of our sexuality, our culture, or our intent.

Moving to rhythm creates trance with little difficulty. As with running, you can push yourself towards limits of stamina and endurance, but it's easier in some ways to dance within your own limits. Slow dancing to soulful music brings as much meditative scope as ecstatic, savagely paced raves. Exploring the relationship between moving and not moving, posture and repetition, grace and bodily mayhem, we can learn ourselves in new ways.

Turning dance into meditation is all about what happens inside your head once your body is in motion. It can be an intense exploration of relationship with self. Barefoot in the open air, dancing can be about moving between the earth and the stars, holding fine threads of connection. Dancing can be an act of communion with gods or ancestors, or an offering to spirits of place. We can dance out our rage, or find the dance of a creature that inspires us. The story of life and identity can be played out through creative movement.

Shared dancing, circle dancing, making spirals of human movement, can create shared trance spaces. My experience so far inclines me to feel that while dancing in the same place works well, dancing for other people doesn't lend itself to meditation. Once you become conscious of what others might think or how they may see you, the experience of dancing changes. We use it so readily for human interaction and courting, that it's too easy to fall back into familiar patterns. If you mean to meditate through dance, then move for yourself, for the land or the gods, but not for the people around you, unless you are sure of sharing intent.

I've danced, music-less by moonlight, slow and strange, for the night and the moon. I've danced in workshops, finding I needed to retreat deep into myself there. I've found moments of intense magic and numinous wonder on the dance floors of seedy night-clubs and the backrooms of pubs. It doesn't matter where you are or how you find your inspiration, it is the giving of self into dance that creates wonder and new awareness.

As with running, dancing spontaneously is something most people don't do. Even in situations where it's socially acceptable to dance, many people still feel awkward about it. Dancing in unlikely places, to the musak in shopping centers, the shrill pips at traffic lights, or in the middle of a car park startles people. I've done that too. Entering a meditative state, it's possible to let go of self-awareness, succumb to the call of the moment and break entirely with convention. To date, this has not resulted in me being arrested, or becoming a social outcast.

Dancing is poetry for the body. Just as any activity can become meditation, so too can any activity be danced. To dance a mundane act as a form of meditation can be both strange and beautiful. The dance need not be overt or obvious, but with small, playful steps, we can dance the supermarket shopping, and turn a banal activity into something profound. We put creativity before convention, and in so doing find freedom and self-expression.

Dancing is also incredibly primal. The first music humans had was the clapping of hands and the making of vocal sounds.

The rhythm of heartbeat is with us from conception, and the power of drums has moved us since prehistoric times. Humans have used dance for ritualized display and courtship for thousands of years. The aggressive street dance forms of today carry the same energies and passions that fuelled our ancestors. Dancing for pleasure, as a social activity creates community cohesion and a sense of belonging. Knowing the same moves, sharing a language of routines and gestures, we belong to the same tribe. It's an essentially human act, ancient, but always vibrant and relevant. When we dance, we dance with our ancestors back into the lost stretches of pre-history. We dance with every shindig, every ball and *ceilidh*. It doesn't matter what music we use, whether we know complex steps or just jump up and down, in dancing we are part of the human tribe, and doing that knowingly is pure magic.

Drumming

Communal drumming comes to us through the same ancient lines of human history that bring us dance. It must have been one of the first forms of music humans discovered, and it is incredibly powerful. The sharing of rhythm and energy that comes from making this most primal form of music is truly intense, and easily accessible to most people. Where physical meditations are concerned, drumming is the one I think that works best for being shared. Drumming on your own is physically demanding, and there's no one to share the workload with. When groups of people drum, it's easier to pause and rest without the whole mood being lost.

It isn't actually important to have drums, there are many other percussive instruments that work just as well, including impro-vised ones. The human body is replete with ways of making noises – clapping, stamping, clicking fingers, banging chests, slapping thighs – we can make all kinds of sounds just using ourselves as instruments. Most environments present things that will make a noise when you hit them together – rocks and sticks work perfectly well. Gathering percussive things from your surroundings is fun and creative, and enables spontaneous drumming. It also draws us into more conscious relationship with our environment. Spoons, pans, cardboard boxes and all manner of other household gear can be appropriated for percussion too.

It isn't necessary to have everyone playing the same thing. I've heard tales of drumming circles that do this – and if it makes you happy then all well and good, but it isn't *necessary*. Nor do people actually need to hold a rhythm. The default of drumming circles tends towards speed and intensity of playing. This is engaging; it makes your blood pump and focuses all attention on the sound. It's exciting stuff and well worth exploring, but it isn't the only option. For some years now, I've been preaching the merits of arrhythmic, ambient drumming. Rather than seeking volume and rhythm, ambient drumming seeks to be as minimal as possible, focusing more on sound than rhythm, working with breaths and silences as well as noise. In gatherings, encouraging people to make minimal sound and to avoid rhythm can be highly effective. It requires attention and focuses people on both the silences and the unexpected combinations of sound. It also means there is space to hear the voice of place as well. Birdsong and wind in trees becomes part of the music created. It's an incredibly moody, thoughtful thing, far more creative and far less physically demanding, so the trance state can be held for a lot longer. It does induce trance, of a very gentle sort, making it ideal for sharing with younger folk. It's easy and inclusive nature lends it to ritual.

While with dancing my experience has been that it works better for me not to engage with other people, drumming is the opposite. When drummers are paying attention to each other, that shared creativity and deepening awareness opens something. I have absolutely no idea why I experience these two forms of physical meditation in such different ways and can see the scope for the opposite being equally true for others. The important thing is to explore what takes you into trance states, and to avoid situations that just distract from what you want to do.

Chanting

Chanting works well in solitary meditation but can become so much more when shared with a group. At its simplest, chanting involves the repetitive use of certain sounds. While some traditions use meaningful words and phrases, and there are some delightful pagan chants out there, it's not necessary to have access to any of these. We can improvise with our voices just as we can with percussion, and to similar effect. However, there is a degree of intimacy in vocal expression that percussion does not create, and this can result in a greater sense of connection between participants.

The Druid chant of preference is the word 'awen' (usually meaning sacred inspiration) pulled out so that it sounds like ah-oo-when and repeated. Tibetan chanting includes a process where you simply move from one vowel sound to another, on any note or notes that occur to you. This is very simple to do, but becomes complex and fascinating when shared. Letting these sounds blend and overlap creates an ever-changing layering of music. As people listen and respond to each other, new sounds and possibilities emerge. As with ambient drumming, you can keep this improvised chanting music loose and free, it only takes a little deliberate chaos to discourage people from defaulting to conventional harmonies and unity. In the shifting patterns of rich discord and individual difference, there is both magic and uncanny music. Being open to this enables our vocalizing to develop deeper levels and affect us emotionally. Using voice in this way is also liberating, helping people shake off inhibition and find self-expression.

The vast majority of people have a voice, and can use it. Group chanting is an easy thing to share so long as someone leads the way. It can be entirely improvised or follow one of the many existing chants. (Brendan Myers book 'A Pagan Testament' includes a large number of circle chants.) The tunes of chants are simple, the words repeated so in principle anyone can invent a chant. Through the repetition of the sound, sometimes words turn into meaninglessness, while at others they acquire a strange life of their own. Concentrating on the chanting makes it difficult to think about anything else, which makes it a good exercise when clearing the mind is needful. If you are overwhelmed with thoughts and chaos and have the space to chant, it can be helpful.

If you pick or write a chant with words that are meaningful and resonant, then they can be used as needed. The verse on fear from Frank Herbert's Dune makes a very good chant, and focusing on words about letting the fear pass over and through is highly effective when trying to get through a fearful situation. Snippets of song lyrics and poetry can be used in exactly the same way, as can the Druid prayers or any other material you can remember and repeat that feels meaningful to you. Words do not need to be sung, only repeated aloud. A whisper will do, but there is something about the act of voicing that makes it different from holding thoughts in your mind. Vocalizing is far more immediate and physical, and keeps the words as a focus where they might be lost amongst other thoughts.

Repetitive Movement
The prolonged repetition of any movement can encourage a trance state. Certain forms of exercise lend themselves to this – some have been mentioned already, but activities such as cycling, swimming, rowing, trampolining, poi, and skipping, all have their own rhythms. How useful these are depends a lot on circumstances – swimming lengths in a local pool you can afford to be somewhat tranced, but in open water it would be

dangerous. Cycling can be incredibly repetitive, as can driving on a motorway at night, but often it pays to resist falling into a trance when not to be fully concentrating invites accident. Once a person is in the habit of entering trance states, it can become if anything, too easy to do so, and it pays to be watchful. If you have control over the space you are in, then using such activities for meditation can be productive, but it should never be under-taken at risk to self or others.

When looking for a form of movement or activity to use for meditation, there are other things you may wish to consider aside from the safety issues.

1) What other benefits, if any, does it bring you? This would include it being good exercise, involving a skill or achieving some other end at the same time.

2) Does it allow you to work creatively or express grace?

3) Do you find it inherently enriching or enjoyable? If not, it's not a good use of your time.

Chapter Three

Meditation for the Heart and Mind

Minds, like bodies, need exercise. If we spend our time on banal tasks and passive leisure pursuits, then our minds atrophy. Like the body, the brain requires attention and nourishment. Where we feed ourselves challenges, seek inspiration and make use of our creativity, life is a lot richer. Creativity is in many ways, a habit to cultivate. Once we become used to thinking, carefully and consciously about our bodies and lives, we can also start to think more about our own emotions, psychological needs and intellectual requirements. Here again, meditation is a tool for awareness, insight and growth.

There is a tendency to see emotion and intellect as entirely separate things. However, for the purposes of this chapter, I'll be moving back and forth between the two. I don't see reason and feeling as polar opposites, nor do I subscribe to the belief that people tend towards being driven solely by one or the other. We do not nurture intellect at the expense of emotion, nor do we abandon reason in embracing feelings. To be a Druid is to seek balance and connection. We can do this within ourselves, connecting our ability to feel with our capacity for thought. When our emotions and reason work in harmony, we gain greater self-awareness and control, improve our capacity for empathy and compassion and lead richer lives.

This section offers workouts for the mind and techniques for developing knowledge of your emotional self. Just as we can be remarkably oblivious to our physical selves, so too we are often encouraged to ignore our feelings and not to think too much. We may feel things that we do not understand or react in ways that make no sense to us, because we have not been paying attention to how we feel. Whether or not we acknowledge emotions, we all have them, and where they are suppressed, they can tangle within us in entirely unhelpful ways.

Emotions can be alarming things – potent, driving, destructive and not always socially acceptable, they are part of our animal selves. To be civilized is to be in control, restrained and not manifesting intense feeling. Showing too much emotion is tantamount to madness. Why have we decided it should be so? Emotion colors and shapes our world, defines our responses and plays a huge part in who we are. And yet we fear it. We hide and contain anything outside a very narrow bandwidth of feelings that seem to be normal and acceptable. In doing this, we throw away the better part of who we could be.

Emotions are also the parents of inspiration. It is our feelings that enable us to create, and drive us to achieve. It is in love, anger, pride, passion, envy, ecstasy, lust, and grief that we manifest our full responses to living. Feelings transform our lives if we let them, taking us out of the monotone shades of grey and into an existence that is bright with color and dramatic with shades of light and darkness. Engaging with emotion means living a life that is intense. It is not an easier life, but it is a far more interesting one. Once we know and recognize our own feelings, they cease to be fearful.

Much the same can be said of our thought processes. We are encouraged to accept the status quo and our own powerlessness, to do what we have always done and to go along with all the conventions around us. 'You think too much' is a criticism I've heard all too often, or 'you take things too seriously.' It may be followed through by a suggestion to 'chill.' This is the only life we get. Every choice we make, every challenge we face, is unique. Every moment is like no other and we only get them once. Thinking about life and self does not reduce scope for spontaneity. It does not necessarily turn you into a worrier or take the fun out of things. It does however move you towards being aware and responsible, conscious of the implications of your actions, and unable to treat anything as trivial, insignificant and worthless. Once you start to think, it becomes hard not to value everything. Especially yourself and the life you have. Not thinking only seems like the easy option if you want to amble through life blind and ineffective, ignoring everything uncomfortable and pretending that you are chilled and having fun. Plenty of people manage it, keeping the fears and hollow uncertainties at bay with noise, alcohol and other intoxicants, dulling their minds with passive leisure activities and meaningless rewards.

Once you enter into silence and permit yourself to think, you begin to hear the quiet voice of your own self. Awareness is a natural consequence – both of who you are, and of all that which you encounter.

Becoming Aware of Moods

People who are not conscious of their own feelings can be surprised by their reactions and perplexed by their own behavior. There are a great many pressures upon us to tune out feelings that are not convenient to others – especially to survive in the workplace. We medicate against melancholy, poor concentration and distress, bury frustration, boredom, anger and disenchantment. If we aren't able to vent flight or fight stresses, those are bottled up too, adding to the uncomfortable mix. It's not socially acceptable to get angry in many circumstances. It's not easy to weep in public unless there's a group grief scenario that is widely understood – chiefly funerals. There are also plenty of situations in which expressions of ecstatic joy are greeted with suspicion as well. If our emotions are inconvenient and unwelcome (as emotions so often are) then there is a lot of pressure to suppress them.

Unable to vent our emotions, it becomes ever harder to even admit them to ourselves. If no one else is drowning in rage and grief at the state of the world, how on earth can we acknowledge that? It isn't normal to weep over the evening news, and so we feel it necessary to respond by toughening up. Somewhere along the line, being an adult was equated with being emotionally controlled and inexpressive. Children are tolerated when they vent, but only because we know they will grow up, and grow out of it. Collectively, we're all still behaving ourselves in the way that production line culture dictates. We bottle up feelings, suppress responses and do not allow ourselves to examine them too closely.

Maintaining the status quo depends on not examining dissatisfaction, depression and frustration. This is utterly subversive territory. To become aware of your actual emotions and to engage with them rather than suppressing them, is to invite change and challenge. We accept so much as necessary, even if it ought to enrage us. To experience those emotions, to encounter righteous indignation, the horror and fury that so much in this life really ought to provoke, is to become someone who will have to consciously work for change. It's rather like that moment in The Matrix. Do you want to know? What would happen to the world if we dared to weep openly over scenes of human suffering? What would happen if we let ourselves feel angry about the state of our neighborhoods and the attitudes of the government? How would it be if we all felt able to express wild ecstatic joy over the good things in life? Everything would change. In re-connecting with our feelings, recognizing our basic right to them, and becoming able to share them, we challenge all the assumptions that hold our materialistic, short-termist, unsustainable and unjust civilization together. This is my Druidry.

Most Pagan and Druid folk I have encountered have already made that choice, stepping out of the mainstream current with its demands and assumptions, to look at other ways of being. It's a choice that radically changes lives. It is the apple of knowledge and it means we can no longer pretend that everything is ok, much less Eden. To be a Druid is to know yourself, accepting that won't always be comfortable.

Self-awareness on the Druid path is not about fuzzy feel good exercises. In knowing ourselves, we inevitably become more aware of all that is around us, sensitive to our own responses and engaging fully with all we encounter. To be self-aware is to be present in the world, and interacting with it. Frequently that isn't comfortable. Discomfort is the price we pay for knowledge. The self does not exist in isolation. This journey into awareness can be a dramatic process of awakening to the world as it is – in all its staggering beauty and cruelty. We sacrifice the ease of denial and willful ignorance. And by so doing, we make it possible to change ourselves, and all that we encounter.

Spirituality, enlightenment, awareness, transcendence – are these things we should seek purely for ourselves? Is it possible to attain some higher state in a world so damaged by human activity and wracked by the cruelties of human abuses? Or, when we work for ourselves, as in meditation, should we be doing so with an intention to do more than stroke our own egos? When we seek our own peace, we can carry that peace to others. What insight and understanding we find, we can use to make a positive difference. A Druid does not seek spiritual advancement purely for their own benefit. We are present in the world and part of it; service is intrinsic to our spirituality. In changing ourselves, we are also seeking to change the world, not as an expression of ego and self-importance, but as a recognition that all is connected, and all change begins from within.

Exercises for Becoming Aware

If you already consider yourself self-aware, and conscious of your own emotional states, these will very likely be simple exercises, useful for sorting through experiences or as warm-ups to more involved meditations. If at this point you do not feel confident that you are already consciously experiencing the full range of your emotions, then give yourself the time and space to approach this work with care.

1) Begin by breathing deeply and settling. Work through a physical meditation if you find this helps. Take the time to be with yourself, and just as you would consider how your body feels, contemplate the state of your own mind and emotions. Are you calm, or are their concerns nagging at you? Are you at peace, or touched by melancholy? Are you hopeful? Inspired? Accept whatever you find – there are no wrong answers, there is only the experience of how it feels to be you at this moment. Give yourself time to be with those feelings, and let them move freely through you. If you wish to, then contemplate their origins as well. This is an exercise to repeat whenever you can. Keep track of how your perceptions of self shift. Are your moods constant or in flux? Are there ongoing issues, or are you simply responding to things as they happen? Do you like and enjoy your own emotions? Why?

2) You can develop the above exercise by reviewing what you have felt over the course of a day. Acknowledge any strong feelings that touched you. Consider if there were moments when you suppressed a feeling, and think about why that felt necessary at the time. Give yourself the space to work through that feeling. You might want to contemplate what you would have done in the circumstances had you felt able. By revisiting the memory, you can reawaken the emotion and give yourself chance to explore it. In this way, suppressed feelings from the day can be explored and brought to the fore. This process of dealing with feelings in retrospect gives us insight, and can often give a degree of resolution, making peace with

the events of the day. It's worth finding the time to do this on a daily basis if you can. The more you are able to engage with your emotions as you experience them, the less time you will need to spend in retrospect. In this process, you will gain insight into which aspects of your life you are happy with, where you draw inspiration, and where you are frustrated or demoralized. What you do with this insight is for you to decide.

3) The process of reviewing can be extended out over your entire life. You might want to review the preceding year, contemplate your childhood, or work through memories by some other means. Again, there is no 'one true way' of approaching this. Understanding your motives, responses and feelings at key moments in your life will help you to make sense of the journey so far, to understand who you are, and make sense of where you need to make changes. This is a process that it is worth undertaking once in a while, but not something to do continually at the expense of being in the present. If it makes more sense to write, draw or otherwise express this, then do so. Having some kind of a record gives you material to return to so you can see how things change, but again, is not something over which to obsess.

4) Working with the insights you gain can take you forwards in all kinds of ways. There are a number of ways of exploring past events. Envisaging how you might have done differently can be productive, but it is important not to become obsessive over details. The point of the exercise is neither to massage your ego nor beat it up – simply to learn who you have been and who you might be. You might want to consider what advice you would give to your younger self if you could go back and

speak to them, and imagine how your younger self would feel about where you are now. Would they be pleased? Encouraged? Horrified?

5) As you become more accustomed to thinking about your feelings, it becomes easier to think as you feel and to be consciously aware of your feelings as they happen. Rather than emotion being a rush that takes you somewhere out of control, it becomes a complex but comprehendible array of things. It's like the difference between hearing an orchestra as one sound, and being able to appreciate each individual instrument at the same time. At first, it may seem unlikely, if not impossible, but we can know ourselves, even in the heat of the most difficult moments. Try to think about your emotions as you experience them, and apply the same approaches to making sense of them as you would when working retrospectively.

6) Being conscious of emotions as they take us, we have a lot more scope for controlling how and where they take us. We don't just have to suppress them in order not to be ruled by them. Think more about which emotional responses you might express. Most people feel more than they ever show. What happens when you are more open? We can also consciously choose how to express our feelings – and this can be incredibly empowering. With the inspiration of great indignation or a passion for justice, and able to speak quietly of it, the scope for affecting change grows dramatically. We can begin days with contemplations of what is to come (based on what we know) and consider how we want to handle it. This becomes an ongoing process, given time, one of prediction and review, and intense awareness of the moments as we live them. It is a process that leaves no

room for apathy or complacency, and that will inspire you to demand the very best of yourself, all the time.

Working with Emotion

Emotions are not our enemies. They are not the antithesis of reason. They have the power to motivate and inspire us, but only if we work with them. In suppressing emotion, we deny ourselves power and creativity. When it comes to being creative, logic and reason are useful, but will only take us so far. The leaps of intuitive insight that turn facts into meanings, the flashes of genius that solves puzzles, are not entirely reasonable.

Creativity is prized in Druidry, and to get the best out of ourselves on that score we need to be able to harness, explore and be led by our own feelings. It is the power of emotion that brings art, poetry and music to life. It is emotion that creates resonance for our human audiences. Working with creativity means not only exploring our own emotions, but contemplating the emotions of others. Empathy is a necessary capacity for all aspects of Druidic work.

Recognizing that all emotion has the potential to be productive, and that all of it has purpose, changes our relationship with ourselves. No emotion needs to be ignored as irrelevant, counter-productive, or unhelpful. How we feel, moment to moment is one of the experiences that tells us who we are. The real, unmasked responses we have to the world matter. Especially when they aren't convenient, don't fit with other people's agendas or seem to take us against the current of the mainstream.

After all, if we do not take our own emotions seriously, we are not taking ourselves seriously. It's important to hold awareness that everyone else is entitled to their own feelings too, and that these may well be different. Our specific, personal emotions should not become a benchmark for normal either.

Exercises for Working with Emotion

1) Once you have settled into a meditative state, pick an emotion to contemplate. Consider times when you have felt that emotion, and what sparked it in you. Emotions rarely turn up alone, so contemplate the other feelings that tend to run alongside the focal one. Allow yourself to experience the emotion, and consider the way you feel it within your body. When you are working with darker or more negative emotions, limit the time you spend on this in any one session, and follow through with something that will restore your sense of balance – such as contemplating a brighter feeling or doing something you find affirming. It is important not to become bogged down or to make yourself unhappy in an ongoing way. It is important to explore both emotions you find comfortable and the ones you do not, and to do so in a balanced way.

2) Contemplate emotions that are not within your normal sphere of experience. For this, you may need to draw on other sources first – such as news or fiction. Firsthand accounts are best. You might watch a news item and try to imagine what the people shown in it are feeling. News tends to focus on extremity, but many people will experience extreme things at some point in their lives. Consider the emotions of the businessman who has just landed a bonus when his employees are being laid off, or the feelings of someone willfully polluting the planet for the sake of short term financial gain. Listen to your politicians and try to imagine how they might feel when they get into bed at night. Look for figures and situations you don't automatically empathize with, and imagine how it would feel to be there.

3) Consider a situation where you have found yourself in disagreement with someone else and try to imagine their feelings, as though you were feeling them yourself. This is a powerful exercise to explore during times of conflict, and is one that will push you towards working for peaceful solutions. Once we start considering how others feel as though we had the same feelings ourselves, it breaks down notions of separation and encourages understanding. Where the problem appears to have come entirely from one side, this exercise can create insight, either requiring us to make reparation, or helping us understand the motives of the one who has distressed us. Sometimes, there is no good or reasonable explanation for the things people do to each other, and it is necessary to face this as well.

Meditation for Intellectual Stimulation

Intellect and emotion both have their place in Druidry. Just as we cannot work without access to emotion, we cannot work without reason either. Reason is a key tool for enabling us to interact with society and other human beings. It is the capacity for analysis, making sense of information, predicting what will happen based on what has gone before. Reason allows us to deduce things when we don't have all the facts, to spot patterns, make connections and process our experience. Intellect enables us to explain and share what we feel, and what intuition suggests to us. Without these things, we do not learn and cannot change. To be a purely feeling creature is to be responsive not active. Emotion may provide the inspiration, but reason gives the tools enabling action. The mind is an organ that benefits from being used on a regular basis and the more we use it, the stronger and more capable it becomes.

Although the language of science and reason dominate the political scene and are widely present in society, we aren't actually encouraged to think. 'Scientists say we have to do this,' is offered as much as a blind faith assertion as any religious instruction. Statistics are thrown at us with no explanation of where they come from. Fear mongers and people with all kinds of political agendas use the language of science to dress up prejudice, propaganda and full on lies. Most people are continually bombarded with messages about who we are supposed to be and what we should want. It's all about keeping us turning as good little cogs in corporate systems, making money for someone else. We're encouraged to want the same as everyone else, live to work, work to pay tax, accept what we are told and express our individuality and choice through the particular brand of thing we select.

Thinking is just as dangerous and subversive as feeling. Thinking enables us to pose questions like 'what is this for?' or 'who actually benefits from this?' When we stop and think, it's much easier to say 'NO' than to be swept along by tides of convention and advertising. Proper thinking requires time, space and quiet. When we're always rushing and surrounded by noise, the voice of reason, like the voice of spirit, doesn't get much opportunity to speak.

'Why?' is such an important question. Children ask it all the time. Adults ought to ask it far more often. If the answer appears to be 'Because it just is,' then the odds are you've just identified something very wrong and probably rooted in injustice, irrationality or both. Why should we take anything on trust? We should be demanding evidence, explanations and reasoning, all the time. And as well as interrogating the apparent authorities in our lives, we need to question ourselves too. Why do we feel as we do? Why do we value certain things? What do we want? Who do we want to be? What kind of world do we want to live in? Once we dare to ask the questions and start thinking, we have a chance of finding some answers.

Meditation does more for us in terms of emotion and imagination than is does to support reasoning and problem solving. However, certain kinds of meditation can be mentally challenging in ways that serve this purpose. Meditation is very good for developing visualization skills, and this can include working with your memories of spaces and entities, sharpening your visual memory and your spatial awareness. Any rational problem can be contemplated from a meditative state, which may prove productive. Those with a fondness for puzzles can create themselves challenges in the form of pathworkings (more on these below.) Creating opportunities for inspiration requires using your intellect to open the way to more intuitive thinking. The process of reflecting on meditations and making sense of them is an intellectual one. It is important to balance the emotional, intuitive experience with deliberate thought.

In the previous section, I talked about using reason to understand emotion. It is also true that emotion colors and informs reason, and gives it purpose. The two are not separate things, but aspects of the same self, the same mind. Dualist thinking tends to separate them out, to categories people as being either feeling or thinking, when really we are, and should be, both. So just as the exercises working with emotion call reason into play continually, so stimulating the intellect is not without emotional aspects.

We can use meditative states to question and explore, to look both inwards and outwards. Making the quiet time that enables thought, we can question everything, and so we should continually. Taking things for granted, assuming things are right because they are 'normal' and going through our days without much thought does not make us self-aware or responsible beings.

Meditative Questioning Exercises

Below are a series of questions you might find it productive to ask yourself whilst meditating. There are no right answers, only your answers. Take one question at a time and sit with it. Skip any that don't seem relevant, but come back to all of them now and then to see what light they shed on your life.

1) Who am I?
2) What do I want?
3) Who do I want to be?
4) Do my actions support who I want to be?
5) What would I change, if I could?
6) What is there in my life that makes no sense to me, and how can I tackle it?
7) Am I carrying any unfounded assumptions about myself, others or any other aspect of my reality?
8) What do I take for granted?
9) What do I do because it is normal and expected?
10) What do I do because I want to?
11) How do I impact on others and my environment?
12) What would I like to achieve?
13) What do I need more of in my life?
14) What do I need less of?
15) What are my priorities?
16) How do I make judgments and choices?
17) Am I using my time in ways that serve my intentions and needs?
18) What would enrich my life?
19) Do my actions enrich the lives of others?
20) What is most important, right now?

As you start asking questions, more will become apparent to you. Questions that directly relate to your self, lifestyle, environment, relationships, work, spiritual path and so forth. If you do not know the answer to something, that is a sign that you need to take it further. The only wrong questions are ones that presuppose the answer, questions like 'why am I so ugly?' are laden with assumption and do not let us make progress. Ask instead 'Why do I have a poor body image?' Avoid questions that are essentially about beating yourself up – everything else is worth exploring.

Once we begin to question, challenge and explore within ourselves, it is easier to do so in the rest of life too. Thinking, like emotion has the potential to be neither safe nor comfortable, but it gives us the power to make changes. Anyone who seeks to control us, or restrict what we think will resent this kind of questioning. Relationships that depend on blind obedience are not healthy or honorable ones, but tackling the consequences of such a realization is more than this book can hope to cover. However, until we recognize a problem, we cannot hope to solve it. The process of asking questions enables us to learn, contemplate, grow and develop. In asking, we can find our own answers a surprising amount of the time.

Opening to Creativity

Creativity and inspiration are not just issues for bards and artists. Creativity enhances all aspects of life. We can think and live creatively, work creatively, bring creativity into our relationships and homes. Inspired choices are far more interesting than ones guided by habit, convention and advertisements.

For some, inspiration appears to be a constant flow, arriving in vast quantities from a mysterious source. Not everyone is automatically blessed with an innate capacity to be endlessly creative. Many people in fact have to work for it, and learn how to open themselves to it. Finding inspiration is in and of itself a skill; that opens the way to all kinds of additional possibilities. It is important to treat all inspiration as equally valid and important – whether it comes in the form of an idea for a great meal, the vision for the theatrical production, or a striking political speech. It's all inspiration, and all merits taking seriously. We might want to judge that inspiration in terms of the effect it has in the world, but that's about its ethical aspect. Inspiration and ethics do not automatically flow together, although for Druids and anyone else with a value system, it is natural to want to combine the two.

Being creative means making the time to find inspiration. There are a great many ways in which we can nourish our own creativity, of which meditation is just one option. Sometimes meditating will bring inspiration without it particularly being sought – a visualization enabling you to connect certain ideas in new ways, solve a problem or see a potential. It's also possible to use meditation deliberately to find creative ideas to work with.

Inspiration Exercises

Here are some simple ways of seeking inspiration. More complex options will be explored in the pathworking section later in this chapter.

1) If you have a form of work you wish to try – such as a painting or a poem, take a moment to contemplate what you wish to achieve. Use your meditation time to settle, employing some of the physical meditation techniques to first create a calm and open mind. Allow your thoughts to wander. Often pushing for creative inspiration doesn't work, when simply being peaceful will enable a little daydreaming, random associations, and bring glimmers of inspiration. Give yourself permission to be still and open, and let whatever comes drift across your mind. Afterwards you can seek to make sense of it and see if you can draw out usable material.

2) You can enhance the above exercise by undertaking it whilst gazing at random, formless things – cloud forms are excellent, flowing water, trees moving in the wind,

flames and so forth. Let your eyes relax into looking at whatever you have picked. See the images within it, the shifting possibilities, and let them remind you of things. Allow yourself to make free flowing associations from what you see until you find the inspiration you need.

3) Once in a meditative state, you can experiment with free word association or doodling, playing random thoughts and ideas onto the paper with no direction or specific intention aside from letting the ideas flow. This can result in seed ideas that can later be developed more consciously. You can work with any medium in this way – recording sound, splodging paint around, playing with clay – and it need not be the medium you ultimately intend to work in. Again it's more about creating a space in which ideas can flow rather than hoping to accidently create something immediately usable.

Sacred Inspiration

Service is a core concept in Druidry. While service to community is relatively easy to find approaches to, service to the land, the ancestors or the Gods is a lot more challenging. How do we know what is needed or wanted? It's all too easy to do what suits us and claim that we do so in service of our deities. Being sure that we are not serving ourselves is therefore difficult. No one is ever going to be able to prove that what they claim as divine inspiration is actually that. However, what we can seek is our own integrity, our own confidence that we hear the voice of spirit, not the demands of ego. Spirit will probably not ask us to go out and be terribly famous and important, to wear lots of dangly jewelry and gather many followers. Service to spirit, in whatever form you understand it, may bring you benefits, but it will also make demands.

We can seek sacred inspiration at any time, and there are

reasons for considering any encounter with awen and inspiration to be inherently sacred. In ritual, we may speak of awen as the divine flow of inspiration, and many Druids see inspiration as a blessing from the gods. The fire in the head, the flash of insight is an inherently magical experience, and we can choose to treat it as such. We can use meditation in ritual, and to seek forms for ritual, we can also use it to bring us closer to the realms of spirit and magical possibility. This is a theme that will be at the heart of the coming chapters.

At this stage, the points to bear in mind are that all meditations can be treated in a sacred way, as manifestations of Druidry, as openings to spirit and as ways of encountering the divine flow of sacred inspiration. The following section is one that opens the way to relationship with all that is around us, and through relationship, we can know sacredness. The more aware we are of something, the more we perceive and appreciate its beauty, uniqueness and spirit. The deeper our relationship, the more important that person, creature, place or thing will seem. The more we know, the more we appreciate. It is possible to see the divine in all things, experiencing all of life as profoundly sacred. Seeing the world in this way changes everything. It can't be taught through a book, but I can tell you it is there, and offer some ways of finding it.

Deep Contemplation of Objects

Any item can be the subject of deep contemplation, but in many ways, it works better if you can hold it in your hand. Having that physical involvement creates greater intimacy and immediacy. Once you are familiar with this practice, moving to things that are more removed, or can only be touched in part, is easier. Any small object will do – natural or manmade. It need not hold any deep significance for you at the outset.

Sit with your object, and hold it as you breathe deeply and settle yourself. Take time to explore the object. Feel the weight of it in your hand and the texture of its surface, the temperature of it. Turn it, explore with your fingers and your eyes. If appropriate, you may wish to smell, lick or taste what you are holding, or to listen for any sounds it makes. Consider what it is and where it came from – if it was made, then who made it and for what purpose? What was it made from? Whose hands has it passed through? If it has come from a living thing – such as a leaf or a feather, then consider where it came from, what life it had and how it arrived in your hands. Consider the seasons and conditions it knew, the way it grew. Think where the future will take your object. Will it rot? Be recycled? Eaten? Consider what it has been made from, and where it belongs in the greater cycles of carbons, water and so forth.

How you approach the next stage, will depend on whether or not you are an animist. If you believe that spirit is present in all things, then the object in your hand will have spirit. If you don't believe this, you may wish to consider what the spirit of such an object might be, or the spirit of the thing it came from. If you find this makes no sense in the context of either your item or your understanding of the world, then skip the next bit and move on.

If you can, contemplate the spirit of the item you hold. Try to sense the energy it has, and listen for a voice. Some things can have voices in an almost human sense and communicate in direct ways; others have tones that are alien to our ears and languages we can only try to intuit. The important thing is to listen and see what comes. If you are not inclined to this more magical approach, you can engage with your object imaginatively, thinking of the kind of voice it would have, the sort of language it might use – this makes a good creative exercise and the two approaches can be run together. It's never easy to determine where imagination ends and intuition begins.

You may want to sit with the same object over a number of sessions, or explore different objects. You might find it interesting to work with a series of similar things – pebbles, twigs from different trees, objects that belonged to different ancestors. Sometimes by comparing different but related things, it is possible to gain additional insight into all of them. Alternatively, ranging over many different kinds of things will give you broader perceptions – both approaches have their uses.

Working deeply with natural objects develops our sense of connection with nature and the elements. When you explore natural items you may also want to consider elemental associations, mythic connections, or any magical traditions associated with the item you have. A little research into the object of your choosing can add dimensions to your meditating with it.

Working with human-made objects is equally valid, and can be an interesting method of shifting perspective. Many of the items around us we take for granted. So many of the things we buy are throwaway; made to be cast aside. Most of the things we own are mass-produced, and not designed to have any character of their own. Yet through use, association and affection the most banal of objects can acquire individuality. Making relationship with the small things in our lives changes our perspective of them.

The stories we have about objects and the journey they share with us transforms the ordinary. The saucepan I inherited from my grandmother is unique to me and irreplaceable, but when it was bought, it was just another pan. What stories are there associated with the things you own? You can sit with the item and meditate upon its story. Why should we make anything only to throw it away? Why should we not see soul and value in the smallest, least important things? Why do we consider some things valueless and pay a small fortune for others? Deep contemplation of disposable goods, of apparently trivial things invites us to change our attitudes in radical ways. Everything has history. Everything came from the earth. To reach for spirit in a tin opener or a plastic wrapper is to enter an entirely different way of relating to everything in your life.

Creative Viewing Exercises

Most of the time, we view the scenes of our lives from the same heights (sitting and standing) and perspectives. Children crawl. They climb under things, hang upside down from things, lie on their backs on the floor to regard the ceiling, and otherwise test their environments. Children explore and play with everything they encounter. The learn to make assumptions about what they are seeing and learn to behave with disinterest like 'proper' adults do. Becoming improper is liberating. Finding that childlike curiosity and capacity for adventure even in familiar places, is another way of re-discovering yourself and your reality. Having a child provides a great excuse for doing the same, but 'I'm meditating' will allow you into the occasional unlikely position as well, if you feel you need to justify doing something eccentric. As adults, we conform to what is expected of us, and treat our spaces in 'normal' ways, which limits how we perceive and understand them. Letting go of those conventions to open to new experience isn't easy.

It's not only children who see the world from different perspectives to adults. Any creatures who share our spaces will view them differently. How does a tree experience a house? How do birds make sense of an office building? Letting go of a human-centric perception opens us to new ways of under-standing and empathizing.

1) If you are able literally to explore your world from different angles, do so. Hang upside down from the sofa. Sit under the table. Lie on the kitchen floor. Choose a position and adopt it, and then contemplate what you can see and how the change of viewing perspective affects your relationship with the space. If you aren't able to do

this, then sit somewhere sensible and contemplate how the space would look from different angles. Try taking your chair to a place you wouldn't normally sit. In front of your television (if you have one) with your back to it will give you a totally different perspective. Sitting on stairs is good – they aren't a place most people tend to stop. I also like doorways.

2) Consider how other entities would experience the space you are in, the angle from which they would view it, how much larger or smaller objects would seem to them, what sense they might make of it. If there are other creatures in your home, start with them. You might also want to consider what your home is like to spiders, and how the creatures living around the outside of it perceive it.

3) Consider how the space experiences itself.

Pathworkings

Of all the forms of meditation, pathworkings are the ones that create the greatest intellectual challenges and require the most creativity. Creating them is an interesting exercise in itself, and running through them gives further scope for creative thinking.

While the meditations we've explored so far focus on fairly simple ideas, pathworkings are much more like a story. They can be as long and involved as you want them to be. However, as with stories they needed to be clearly bounded by beginnings and endings. Pathworkings can be carried out solely for flexing your creative muscles. They can be constructed to explore specific issues, for example working through something that you are afraid of. They can help you unlock your inspiration. They can also be used for sacred purposes.

To a large extent, the pathworking is a journey into your own mind. But it is also possible to relate to it in other ways. How do we define 'real'? Inner realities are important, and they do affect outer ones, a fear overcome in a pathworking, may well be a fear overcome in the rest of life. We can't prove that where we go in deep meditation is anywhere but the depths of our own minds. Yet sometimes, ideas and energies so unexpected and unfamiliar come to us that it seems easier to believe they have an external source. There can be no hard rules about how to tackle this issue, and more often than not, it will come down to intuition and personal belief.

Here are some things to bear in mind however. Whatever you lean or think you know from an external source, you are still responsible for how you handle that insight and how, if at all, you act upon it. Anything and anyone can be wrong. If an entity appears to be asking something dishonorable of you, then it may not be what you thought it was, or it may be testing you. In all things, your sense of honor is the only guide you have. How you act in a pathworking is a manifestation of how you are, and who you are.

Some traditions hold the idea that what we think is as real as what we do, so that to imagine killing someone is just as great a wrong as actually killing someone. Other, more conventional ways of thinking incline towards the idea that what we do in our own heads is private, and entirely separate from what we do in actual reality. Again, this is a matter of personal belief because we cannot objectively know. However, if you've never considered killing your neighbor with an ice pick, the odds of you waking up one morning and doing just that have to be lower than if you think about it every day. Actions are born of thoughts and intentions. The ideas we focus on and nourish are the ones that will influence us. In choosing what we think about and contemplate doing, we do choose who we are. If we choose to focus on anxious and depressing thoughts, we will be less happy than someone who avoids them. We may also be more realistic. Someone who avoids thinking about the unhappiness around them is unlikely to be able to change things for the better.

Sample Pathworkings

The following section offers some examples of pathworkings with which to experiment. An explanation of how to write your own will then follow. Each pathworking also includes some notes on the meditation and aspects that you might want to mull over afterwards. A more detailed section on pathwork analysis follows, but this will give you a place to start.

These are complex meditations that need prior planning. You can either record the words of the pathworking inserting suitable pauses, or you can learn the gist of it and work it through from memory. I would advise against working from the written version because opening your eyes to study it will detract from the process. Learning the narrative thread of a pathworking without starting to imagine yourself undertaking it, is tricky but possible. You might want to keep a diary to record your pathworkings and experiences of them, but it's by no means necessary. In group meditation scenarios (discussed later in the book), there is the possibility of having one person lead the pathworking while everyone else is free to imagine it. This is the optimal way of doing it – you have structure and the narrative flow without having to organize it yourself, and the advantage of surprise, which makes the experience more immediate. Solitary pathworking is entirely viable and can be highly rewarding.

Before you begin any pathworking, settle yourself – sitting or lying down is best, in a position you can comfortably maintain. Make sure you are unlikely to suffer interruptions, turn off phones and other unnecessary technology and then proceed.

1) Close your eyes and go deeply into yourself, until you are calm and your thoughts are settled. Imagine that you are walking down a woodland path. Trees surround you,

light filters through branches, birds are singing. Look for signs that tell you what time of year it is. Listen to the crack of old twigs beneath your feet, smell the scent of trees and leaves. At last, you come into a clearing. It is a friendly, welcoming place, surrounded by ancient and beautiful trees. Take time to consider each tree in turn, and to sit at the center, feeling the grove holding you. If anything comes to you in this place, then welcome it. Otherwise, simply be here, observe and allow yourself to experience. When you are ready, then leave the grove and find the path back through the woodland. Follow the familiar path, back out of the otherworld, back towards yourself. Allow yourself to become aware of your body again, as it is here and now. Be aware of your breathing, and then return fully to yourself and open your eyes.

The sacred grove meditation as described above is widely regarded in Druidry. It's a very simple pathworking, and well worth exploring. More of the possibilities and implications of this exercise will be considered in the next chapter. As there is no real narrative to this pathworking, you can revisit it and have entirely different experienced on each occasion.

2) Take the time to slow your breathing and find a calm state. Relax into the quiet of deep meditation. Once you have settled, imagine that you are walking down a stone staircase. There are torches burning on the walls, and the air is cool. All is quiet as you descend but you can hear each footfall. At the bottom of the stairs, you find three doorways. Each door is beautifully carved and ornate. On the first door is the word 'past' the second says 'present' and the third says 'future'. Pick one of these doors, step through it, and see where it takes you. When you have seen enough, return to the door, and make your way back

up the stone stairs, back to your body and your self-awareness until you are ready to open your eyes.

You can go back and explore the other doors in later meditations. It works best only to tackle one at a time. If you revisit the same door, you may well have entirely different experiences.

3) Enter your deep, meditative state. Imagine that you are walking up a steep rocky path through the mountains. To your right, the ground falls away into a ravine, and far below you, a river runs. Steep rock rises on the far side of the river. Listen to the sound of the water, feel the rocks beneath your feet as you climb. Be aware of the wind. This is a hard path with loose stones and the drop is precarious, but you are climbing none the less. At last, you reach the top, take a moment to relish the achievement and look back at the view. What can you see behind you? When you are ready, carry on. Before you, there is a bridge. A figure steps out from behind a rock, halting between you and the bridge. You recognize this person at once as a friend, they wear symbols familiar to you and their smile is welcoming. The figure greets you and tells you that you have done well to reach this point. 'Now you must cross the bridge' you are told, 'but in the center of the bridge you will meet with your own fear.'

The bridge spans the ravine, and far below the river rushes. You step out onto the bridge, and begin to cross. As you approach the center of the bridge, you find your fear waiting for you. What form does it take? How will you pass it? How will you overcome it to reach the other side?

Once you have crossed the bridge, you find the path becomes easier and the views stretch out for many miles in all directions. You come to a little stone house carved into the side of the rock. It's cool inside, and as your eyes adjust to the gloom, you see an object on the floor. Something you know you were meant to find. Pick it up and examine it. If you want to, you may take it with you. You emerge from the stone house to see the way before you clearly marked. You follow the path, down a gentle incline towards a restful landscape, but all the while as you walk, you are returning to yourself, coming back to your awareness of yourself as you are now.

It is possible to become stuck on the bridge with this scenario, if you find a fear that you do not know how to overcome. If this happens, then return the way you came and bring yourself out of the pathworking. You might want to try it again another time. Interpreting the fear is usually straightforward enough – although if you encounter something unexpected you might want to consider that at greater length. The object you find at the end of the pathworking may be something to contemplate, and there may be additional details in the person you meet and the landscape that have wider significance for you.

4) Take as long as you need to settle into a relaxed and meditative state. It is a warm summer's day and you are walking through a beautiful garden. Around you, there are flowers in profusion, you can smell the rich aroma of their scent, and you can hear the soft buzz of bees. This is a garden full of nooks and secret places, hidden seats, secluded corners, statues, fountains. Take some time to explore it and see what you find. After a while, you see in front of you a long tunnel of trees. Go forward towards the tunnel. The trees grow thickly, their branches inter-twining above you. Beneath them the ground is thick with leaf litter. It's cool and shady here. The trees are ancient and gnarled, but very beautiful. You walk

through the tunnel of trees, and when you come to the end, you see a little, secret garden, surrounded by a high hedge. At the center of this garden is a plinth, on which stands a large bowl. Walk over to the bowl. At first, you will see the sky reflected in it, but as you draw closer, you will be able to see your own reflection. Pause for a while and look at what you see of yourself.

You see the image in the bowl change, the waters swirl and your reflection vanishes. In its place, you see a different scene. Gaze into the bowl and watch what unfolds.

The waters cloud again, the image fades until you are gazing once more at your own reflection with the sky above you shining in the bowl. The water looks cool and inviting. Dip your fingers into it. If you taste the water, you will find it sweet and refreshing, cooling away the warmth of the day and leaving you invigorated. When you have spent enough time with the bowl, turn away from it and go back to the tunnel of trees, walk along that shady corridor between the gnarled trunks, back to the rest of the garden, and when you are ready, come back from the garden, back into yourself, and open your eyes.

You might find all kinds of interesting things in the garden, and if you are ever sidetracked by an unexpected encounter in such a pathworking, go with it – often it pays not to stick to the plan when something interesting comes along. You may not see yourself as you literally are when it comes to examining your reflection. Some people find it very difficult to picture themselves. What you see may tell you something.

The Pathworking Narrative
It is not difficult to write a pathworking. In essence, you are putting together the bones of a short story in advance and then

playing through the precise details imaginatively. You can use any setting at all for a pathworking – familiar places, be they urban or rural, historical scenes, fantasy scenarios, situations drawn from myth or story. Anything that you find resonant, helpful or interesting is available for you to explore. As the majority of Druids work very much with nature, then taking natural settings often makes most sense to us. However, there are Druid groups who work specifically with the modern myths from science fiction and fantasy as well. There are Druids whose work is inherently urban. You may wish to work imaginatively with an ancient site, imagining yourself walking a ceremonial path, or approaching Stonehenge as it was when first built. Your imagination can take you anywhere. All places and times are yours to contemplate.

This is primarily written for someone creating pathworkings for themselves, but much of this also applies to meditations designed for groups – the basic structure and points are exactly the same regardless of the number of people involved.

Every pathworking begins with a settling exercise. The examples I've given include a brief 'get yourself into the right place' instruction, because by now you should know how to do that. If you're writing pathworkings for other people, you may not be able to assume that degree of experience, and will need to talk people through the settling phase in more detail.

There then needs to be a short opening section that allows you to place yourself in the scene. At this point, it makes sense to focus on sensory details – take the time to think about all of the possibilities for sound, scent, sight, touch, taste and perhaps also what you are intuitively aware of. This aids the transition from regular thinking into pathworking scenario. It can also be a great deal of fun and may provide inspiration or insights as well.

The central section of a pathworking should open you up to following your own inventions. It needs a situation, an encounter, or a challenge for you to engage with. It's the middle of your narrative, where the action happens. That might be as simple as sitting in a glade and seeing what comes to you; looking into a mirror, choosing a door, crossing a bridge, opening a box to find an object or navigating around a physical obstacle. You can draw on myth and story for these – the black knight at the crossroads, the strange old wizard who asks awkward questions ... there's an infinity of possibilities to imagine and explore. You need to plan what the central section will be about, but don't plan the details, and never include any significant instruction about how to handle the situations you design. Give yourself plenty of time and freedom to do that in the meditation. This is where you have most scope to be creative as you are meditating, so give yourself as much room to move as you can, framed by something that will stimulate your mind, engage your emotions, or both.

You can extend a pathworking session by stringing multiple encounters into a single exercise, but it's easier to remember shorter plans, and there are advantages to not spending too long meditating in one go – you are less likely to be disturbed, for a start. It also makes post-meditation analysis easier if there aren't too many elements to think over.

At the end of the pathworking, it is important to have something that helps you resolve the situation and move away from it. Some people recommend beginning the pathworking by walking down a stair and ending it by walking back up – this has the benefit of being easy to remember, but it does conceptually set the mid section underground, and I found that didn't work when I wanted to relate to something very much here and now. Picking an affirming action to round off the pathworking – as with the drink of water in exercise 4 – can help complete the meditation in a positive way. Having a situation where you walk back down the mountain or out of the forest works well. Where possible, it pays to pick a pathworking where you can go into a space, and come out of it by the same or similar route. Avoid jolting out suddenly if you can – it can be disorientating.

Once you've completed the pathworking, give yourself a few minutes to settle back into 'reality' – don't hurry. You may want to do some stretching and bending to get yourself properly comfortable in your body. Take a few minutes to review the pathworking, and if you are keeping a diary, now is the time to make notes. If the pathworking leaves you in any way disorientated, then food and drink are always the best remedy.

A pathworking can be revisited, and it's interesting to see how differently they play on later attempts.

When you are writing a pathworking, the details you leave out are at least as important as the ones you mention. It is necessary to leave plenty of gaps for your imagination to play in, and so if you try to describe every detail of, say, the walk into the wood, you don't actually get as much benefit from the meditation itself. You need to start with strong sensory details to get into the pathworking, but then it often pays not to have clear instructions of what to perceive, but questions. Ask yourself how it tastes, feels, smells, and let the answers come in the working. Often it's these details that give away critical things about our inner states and that set our imaginations free.

Whether you record your pathworking and play it back, or learn it by heart, the pauses in fixed narrative are as important as the words you plan. In some ways, it's easier to do a guided meditation like this with an experienced practitioner leading the way and managing the timing, but that's not always an available option. Working alone, you have to figure out the timing for yourself, and looking at a clock ruins the flow. There's always the possibility of over running, falling asleep, or being disturbed part way through. However, being entirely in control of your own pathworking means that you can decide exactly how much time you want to spend working through each envisaged experience.

Some pathworkings don't work. It might be that they don't suit your mood on the day, or they contain something too hard to picture. This is not a problem, just something from which to learn. Failure is an experience in its own right and teaches as much as success does. If something doesn't work for you, there is nothing inherently wrong with that, or with you. Either try it again and see if it goes differently, or move on.

Frequently these deep and extended meditations gain a life of their own. Random details leap in, bringing inexplicable images, unexpected tangents, and sometimes a total loss of plot. This is fine too, and does in fact constitute a successful pathworking. The pre-planned narrative is there to give you a place to start. If you follow it through and gain something, that's excellent. If it transforms as you do it and becomes something else entirely, that's fine too.

When you begin to experiment with writing pathworkings, it's best to start small and work up. Begin with things you can easily picture, and emotional content you aren't going to find too difficult. As your confidence with this meditation form grows, you can create more complex settings, stories and challenges.

The exercises in this section are, for the greater part about building confidence with visualization, exploring inner landscapes and working with the self. However, the same tools can be used to approach meditation for spiritual reasons. We can consciously seek guidance, connection and insight through meditation, which is where the next chapter will go.

Analyzing the Pathworking

The work of a pathworking does not end as you emerge from your meditation. This is the point at which you have to decide what you want to do with the experience. Each pathworking will be different. Some prove to be fun, but not especially meaningful.

If the exercise was undertaken with the intention to de-stress, then there might not be much to do aside from deciding if it worked or not. Where a pathworking is undertaken to seek inspiration, you then have to gather up your thoughts and see if you can make something from them.

As with dreams, pathworkings can be analyzed for what they tell us about our inner states. And as with dreams, this is a complicated business. I don't personally believe that there is some dictionary of symbols where one thing found in dream or meditation can be equated to another thing. I do not believe that the unconscious sends us simple coded messages drawn from a great big, shared book of codes. However, what bubbles up when we meditate is full of symbolism, of the peculiar, semi-intuitive language our unconscious mind uses to try to communicate with our conscious selves.

Sometimes there are things we know, or feel, that we refuse to allow into our conscious minds. I lived with carefully suppressed fear for many years and it emerged in a continual barrage of anxiety dreams about running away, and failing exams. I ignored it for all the reasons I was suppressing the fear. In much the same way, people suppress all kinds of emotions. If you are conscious of your feelings then weird dream messages are less likely to happen to you. If strange imagery or recurring themes pepper your pathworkings, it may be that there are issues you need to face and resolve. Only you will be able to unpick your dream/meditation symbolism. I find it helps to focus on the emotional content – because those are usually true, even if the contexts they play out in seem nonsensical. Fear and anxiety manifest as themselves, even if you are running away from haunted table clothes and facing math exams written entirely in Greek.

Be careful about pushing too hard for meaning. If no obvious insights present themselves, don't try to force an interpretation. This is not a test; you do not lose points for coming out of it with nothing specific. The experience is valid and useful whether or not it affords direct and obvious insight. With enthusiastic over analysis, it is possible to turn anything into something it wasn't. I used, for the amusement of friends, to do Freudian style dream analysis, where the game was to turn the key content of the dream into sexual symbols and then somehow twist them into a justification for something Oedipal. It makes an entertaining game, but also serves as a useful demonstration. Any meaning can be read into any experience if you are determined enough, but this isn't always helpful and is often the opposite.

Chapter Four

Meditation for Spiritual Purposes

While meditations can be undertaken purely for bodily, emotional or intellectual purposes, they can also be used for spiritual explorations. Meditation does not define Druid practice, but the exercises in this section explore Druidic concepts using meditation as a way in. Not everyone would relate to these ways of working as being inherently meditative or approach them from this direction. For these purposes, meditation is simply a tool that allows a solitary person to explore some aspects of Druidic practice. The concepts and exercises offered here are by no means definitive of Druidry, nor are any of them necessary for following a Druidic path. Take what makes sense to you, discard anything that feels counterintuitive, and re-write wherever you find it necessary. If you can see another way of doing things, then try it. Any exercise that can be approached from a different angle, subverted, upended and otherwise shaken, is fair game for just such endeavors. There are no right answers here; only tools that may prove useful.

The purpose of any spiritually motivated meditation, is in essence, connection. The meditations explored in previous chapters were very much about the self. This is an important grounding. Self-awareness is necessary in a spiritual life. How are we to know anything else if we do not know ourselves? However, spirituality is more than self-knowledge, and making connections beyond ourselves is very much part of Druidry.

How do we go about making connections with things that are not human? Or, human entities so removed from us that we will not make immediate sense to each other? How do we form relationships with the land or with trees, creatures, buildings or deities? For someone grounded in rationalistic modern perception, the whole notion may seem impossible, if not insane. But in truth, whether we notice them consciously or not, we have relationships with the land and sky, the food we eat and the air we breathe. Our lives are built of subtle connections, dependencies and relationships. Part of the work here is to understand those.

In exploring our own bodies and minds, and especially in working with the elements we become conscious of those more functional connections. Moving into a spiritual approach to meditation, these are exercises to revisit, viewing those connections not just as practical necessities, but also as inherently sacred. Druidry is a shift in perspective away from seeing all things as mundane, towards seeing all things as meaningful and rich with spirit. It is this perception shift that enables a person to then go forward and work with spirit.

Connecting with the Land

For me, Druidry begins with the land, and with recognition of its sacred, magical nature. The spirit of the place we are in, the spirit of the earth that holds us, and the spirits who share the land with us are all part of this same discovery. In knowing the land, we know where we are, and are much better placed to know who we are. The land sustains us, and we owe our existence to it. Our duty of service includes a responsibility for the land we inhabit.

The idea of 'land' may suggest pristine nature, or rural idyll. Perhaps it conjures up images of mythic pasts and epic landscapes, the views on picture postcards. If the spirit of the land sounds to you like it belongs in Tolkien, or perhaps the remote Highlands of Scotland and the environs of Stonehenge, then pause for a moment. All land is sacred. It's not just ancient sites and remote 'other' places that are part of the land. Everywhere counts. No matter where we are, there is land beneath us somewhere. It may have a lot of concrete and tarmac on it, but it is not less present for that. Recognizing that here, where we are, is sacred and can be related to as such is the critical point from which all else follows. If we hold any sense that sacredness is somewhere else, somewhere 'special' then we miss what is most immediate to us.

Connecting with the land begins simply by being upon it, and being conscious of our presence upon the earth. Those walking and running exercises of the first chapter are acts of connecting with the land. Go outside. Get off the cement and tarmac is you can because that's easier when you're starting out. Find a place where there is grass or soil beneath your feet so that the land itself is more apparent to you. You will find that there is a huge qualitative difference between how it feels to walk directly upon the earth and how it feels to have a man-made substance beneath you. Take the time to walk mindfully, and feel the earth beneath you through the soles of your shoes. Walking with awareness of the earth beneath you is a powerful meditative exercise in its own right.

You can bring other parts of your body into contact with the ground by sitting or lying upon it, pressing your hands against the soil, or going barefoot. Creating a tangible, physical connection helps increase your awareness of the land.

Walking barefoot creates an intense awareness of the ground, and as you experience the textures and temperatures directly, they will tell you much about the surfaces you are walking over.

The land may be a single thing, but each corner of it has its own specific character and identity. Connecting with the land is different wherever you stand. The shape of the earth, the nature of the soil, the history within it and the life currently upon it varies wildly. Take the time to observe these nuances.

You can approach the land in similar ways to thinking about physical objects, touching, feeling, imagining and contemplating, blending your rational knowledge with intuition. I like to think about the taste of soil, the weight and texture of it. I've lived on heavy clay, on lighter loams, camped on all kinds of ground. Lying close to or directly upon the earth, the scent of it discernable as is the weight or its vastness against my own relatively small presence. All that we are comes from the earth, and in the end, we return there. In morbid moments, I've explored meditations on my own decay, envisaging the inevitable crumbling of my body and its return to the vibrant life of the soil. I find this kind of imagery soothing, but suspect not everyone would.

Close to the earth, deep in a meditative state, it is often enough just to be open and to listen. Do not expect words or coherence, or anything that makes immediate rational sense, but in listening to the earth, and opening to the land around us, we begin a process of growing awareness. A sense of the soil and our connection to it grows with a repeated, conscious searching for it. A feeling of rootedness gives us some protection from life's continual buffeting and uncertainty. No matter where we find ourselves, we can hold that sense of belonging. Some lands will turn out to speak more directly than others. Certain places hold our hearts, and others prove hard to engage with. It is all part of the process of learning our own natures and those of the spirits we encounter.

In urban settings, the land is still with us, even when we can't see it. With time and mindfulness, holding a sense of the land beneath the tarmac is possible. There may be layers of human history and archaeology under our feet as well. Where humans have lived for a long time, the bones of the ancestors are very much part of the earth beneath us, such that there may be little point trying to think of them as separate. Urban spaces are not all hard surfaces and man-made substances. Once you start looking, there's a lot of soil visible in gardens and parks. Trees and shrubs crop up in the urban environment – wild ones creeping into the cracks, others that have been planted decoratively. Green verges on the sides of roads, exposed dirt in building sites, planters full of imported dirt in public spaces ...

However thick the concrete may seem, the human layer placed on the soil is nothing like as deep or as old as the earth beneath. The contours of the land still show through in the shapes of streets. Watercourses flow in pipes beneath pavements, and over drain covers in wilder weather. Many urban areas grew up in response to river crossings and other natural elements of the environment. Cities are not separate from nature. They have been influenced by it and they exist within it. The land is no less present in towns and cities; it's just somewhat less obvious.

For an urban Druid, making a relationship with the land does not mean having to go somewhere else. If you've chosen to live in a place for pragmatic reasons, such as cost, transport and employment,, or you prefer the social opportunities and buzz, recognize that choice and honor it. Your Druidry does not have to be about being somewhere else. Be led by what inspired you to be in this place. Honor the energies that nourish you, and seek the green amongst the greys as part of the environment you are in.

In urban environments, try contemplating what the land would have looked like before people started building. Was it rock, or river mud? Were there marshes, forests, or moorlands? Sometimes the place names offer clues about previous land uses. Through the history of a city, the uses of spaces will have changed. Villages are gobbled up by expanding urbanization, leaving a legacy of place names, the occasional patch of green, and the remnants of school, pub and church that once represented whole communities. The history of urban places is there to be found – through conventional research, looking at what you can find, and listening with heart and feet to the flow of the land beneath the tarmac.

As you walk the streets, picture the land around you as it might have been, with the creatures who would have inhabited it in centuries, or millennia passed. Seeing the wildworld in the urban, gives a different perspective, shows the recent, transient nature of human structures. They seem so present and overwhelming, but look around and you'll see where older ones have succumbed to time. Nature reclaims unmaintained roads, takes back the railway sidings and clambers over anything we build.

Working indoors and connecting with the land may seem a touch peculiar and counter-intuitive. On the whole, I'd advocate getting as close as you can to whatever you want to work with. However, weather conditions, constraints of time and physical issues may all make working outside challenging at times. It's better to do what you can than to do nothing at all. I recommend working indoors with the land that is actually beneath you, and the landscape that would have pre-dated your building. Even if you are several stories up in a flat, that building still has its foundations in the land.

There are some teachers and courses who suggest working meditatively with more distant sites you are not able to visit in person. You may also find yourself invited to work with entirely imagined settings. There is nothing inherently wrong with this, but different work serves different purposes. Be clear about why you want to do a thing, and what kind of experience you are looking for. There are differences between imagining and doing, they are separate experiences, although both have value and validity. My personal preference is for doing, and I will seek actual experience over imagination whenever I can. I find this makes my ability to imagine a lot stronger because I am nurturing it with reality.

No doubt, part of my bias towards getting outside and actively engaging with the world comes from the fact that I can. I am physically able and have only ever lived in places where I could venture out safely on my own. I am aware that not everyone has these options. If life has limited you and does not allow you to wander where you wish, then tools of the mind are the ones you must depend on. However, do not opt purely for imagination. The place you are in, and the land beneath it, are as much a part of the earth as any other and can be your real, rooted basis for working.

Connecting with Other Living Things

What other living things are a part of your life? Take a moment to consider the creatures who live around you – in your home and outside it. What about the ones who are affected by your presence, whose lives or habitat are implicated in your food? Consider the living things you pass whenever you are out.

To make connection, you first need recognition. Take the time to be aware of the other lives within your life, human and non-human alike. Make a point of looking for them; notice the plants around you as distinct individuals. Where you can, take the time to stop and look. We are never alone. There is always something else in proximity to us.

Although we may not think consciously of these as relationships, they still exist. Everything we affect or come into contact with, we have relationship with. By being more aware of those other lives, we can choose the shape of the relationship. Take the time to contemplate this and make it part of your daily awareness. If you quietly greet other living things as you would a familiar person, how does your sense of them change? You may also want to reflect on how your sense of self, changes in response to this shifting of awareness.

We humans tend towards a very human-centric view of the world, prioritizing 'us' and anything that looks like us. Recognizing all life as sacred changes our relationship with it. We still have to eat, and part of the reality of living is that other things die to enable this. We have as much right to eat as anything else does. However, we do not have the right to waste, spoil for our own amusement, or destroy anything that happens to be inconvenient. Not only do we put human life first, but our society places financial growth before respect for other living things. As a culture we treat money as sacred, not life, and this urgently needs to change.

Becoming more aware of other living things as entities in their own right creates conscious relationship with them. In so doing, it becomes harder to see them as things that exist solely for our use or convenience. The money-worship that drives people to sacrifice yet more precious habitat and push yet more creatures towards extinction is only possible when you do not care. If money is the only thing that matters, everything else can be burned on its altar as required. To what end? A life that does not allow you to care for anything real, is a lonely, empty and hollow sort of existence that no number of shiny toys is ever going to make up for.

As with land-orientated meditations, I would recommend using these exercises in proximity to that with which you wish to connect. In many ways plants are the easiest non-human entities to work with, because it's easy to predict where they are going to be, and unlike other creatures, they stay helpfully still. And so it is with plants that we begin.

Exercises for Connecting with Plants

Choose a plant with whom you can sit. If you need to be inside, then work with a potted plant, or with something close to your window. There's much to be said for doing this outside with a plant in its natural environment, if possible. However, plants in greenhouses are also possibilities. You might want to consider whether the plant arrived there by chance or was planted by someone. Does the method or location of planting affect the plant? Do you need a wild forest to truly connect? There is definitely a great deal of difference between being in woodland with a tree, and being on the side of a busy road with a tree. It's worth giving yourself opportunity to compare the two.

If you can work within the bustle of urban spaces, there is every reason to connect with urban trees. Their beauty makes so much difference to towns and cities. Urban trees are often brutalized into convenient shapes, but where they are allowed to keep their natural form, can be as lovely as their wild counterparts. They provide shade, attract birds and enrich urban areas, but many people hardly seem to see them at all. Becoming aware of them adds a lot to life in built up places.

Working with plants that you are inspired by, and focusing upon them will create deeper connections and insights. For example, mistletoe has a lot of history and mythology associated with it, making it a very attractive plant. You might equally be inspired by scent, visual beauty, herbal applications, or the name the plant has been given. You might find the way it grows affects you – the sheer tenacity, survivability and flexibility of willow profoundly inspires me, for example.

Working with what is immediately around you will reinforce your relationship with the land. That might mean your garden, or a scrap of land nearby. If you have access to a wood or park, this might be the place to go. Alternatively, you might want to adopt the bench under an urban maple and spend time exploring its peace in the hubbub of city life.

While you might choose to focus intensely on one or two plants, you might be more inclined to spread your workings over an assortment of plants, exploring herbs and trees, wild and domesticated, the young, the mature, the dying. Plants have their life cycles too; some are only fully present for short seasons. Seeking connection with a range of plants in different places will bring a breadth of experience. There's no single right approach to this, simply do what makes most sense to you.

Working meditatively with plants, supports working practically with them. You may well find that meditative work changes how you relate to plants in other contexts. If you have a garden, then you can meditate with it. That might just mean sitting in it, but it can mean taking your open, mindful approach into planting, weeding, watering, and harvesting.

If you are buying fresh plant matter as food, you can meditate with it too. Being more aware of plants can make it much more appealing to be close to the whole food and working with it that way. It's not easy to feel any relationship with food that comes out of a tin or packet, whereas the processes of cleaning, cutting and cooking give us a greater sense of the plant as both a life form in its own right, and a source of food. It's not a comfortable thing to waste such food when you have a consciousness of it's aliveness and individuality. We live in a culture that throws good food away in obscene quantities. A greater respect for plants and animals alike would change this.

If you are using a place for magical reasons, then meditating with its land and plants will help in this process. If you need to work with a plant for medicinal reasons, then working with it on this level too may be productive for you as well. The more deeply involved we are with what we do, the more power it has to affect change.

Eating a plant is a way of connecting with it. To eat, in full meditative awareness, creates profound gratitude for the energy given, and for the life of the plant. Any act of working with plant matter – planting, tending, harvesting, foraging, woodcutting, sculpting, pruning and so forth, can be treated as a physical meditation and used to deepen relationship with the plants.

1) Sit or stand with your plant. Take the time just to be with it, look at it, seeing it's individuality. You might want to

sniff it, touch its surfaces (although not all plants are suitable for this, make sure you know!) Contemplate the land in which the plant lives and how it is part of its surroundings. What kind of soil nourishes it? What climate does it experience? What lives near it or upon it? Take time to be with the plant and gain some sense of its existence. Think about the life cycle of the plant and the stage you are seeing. Consider how the current season affects it and how it will change over the months to come.

2) When you sit with your plant, imagine that you are the same kind of plant. Think how your roots would feel in the soil. Are they deep, or shallow? How would you experience the environment around you, from this stationary position? What feed upon you, and what nourishes you? Visualize yourself as rooted in this place, part of the landscape, holding the same form. Imagine yourself with leaves.

3) Listen to the plant. Be open to its presence. Try to sense the energy and life of the plant. Accept whatever comes to you. Don't go into this exercise seeking words or wisdom, especially not messages for your own life.

4) (This is a good 'at home' exercise). Go as slowly as you can, because plants are slow, the fastest ones take a long time to move by human standards. Imagine that you are a seed in the soil. Feel your solidity, the dark dampness around you. Consider the taste of the earth. What will make you germinate? Is there sunlight, or does it grow warmer? Picture yourself putting up that first shoot, and extending roots down to seek for moisture. Grow towards the sunlight. Unfurl your leaves, feel the rain and the sun upon you. Feel the wind stir you and the

insects come to you. You might want to imagine your plant self through a cycle of the seasons, or through the life cycle of the plant. You can do this sitting with the plant, or you can do it at home.

5) The spirit of a plant is not always the same as its outward appearance. If you are working deeply with a specific plant, you may wish to enter a meditative state, and contemplate the plant's spirit. Ask the plant if you can meet it in spirit form. You may wish to set yourself up a pathworking into the right environment to meet with the plant spirit. If you are also working medicinally, you may wish to speak with the plant you have been recommended to take.

6) If you are seeking for inspiration or soul healing, you may wish to find a suitable plant to work with. You can use meditation and pathworking to ask for guidance on a spiritual level. Unless you are confident as a herbalist, be careful how you work with plants in a physical way responding to meditative insight. If the plants recommending themselves to you are culinary, then you are undoubtedly safe to eat them. Otherwise, research the plant by conventional means to find out how best to use it, or seek advice.

7) Working with edible plants gives you very direct ways of experiencing them. Take a piece of plant matter that you can safely eat – such as an apple, slices of carrot, or a sprig of herbs. Hold it in your hand as you would with any other physical object. Feel the weight and texture of it. Consider where the plant grew, the soil it inhabited, the seasons it grew through and the life it will have known. Taste it and take the time to really consider that taste and

how your body responds to it. Taste the sunlight that nurtured it, the water that swelled it and the soil in which it grew. Taste the life in it, and feel that life enter your body. Feel it become part of you. Think of the spirit of the plant as you consume it. Offer gratitude for its life and take a moment to consider the way in which life moves from one being to another.

8) Carry a small piece of wood or dried plant matter with you in a pocket. Handle it, from time to time, be aware of its presence, listen to it, explore it and allow it to become a part of your life and experience.

9) Contemplate how plants relate to each of the elements. You may wish to explore the relationship between one plant and all of the elements, or take each element in turn and contemplate how different plants relate to it. Earth is relatively easy, for plants are of the earth, and usually rooted in it. All plants are nourished by water, and some grow in it. Non-water dwelling plants reach into the air, and contribute to it, absorbing carbon dioxide and releasing oxygen. Many use the air for pollen distribution, or depend on winged creatures to assist them in reproduction. Most plants burn, but some have complex relationships with fire, needing it to facilitate their regeneration. Sun is also fire, and most plants depend upon it to enable photosynthesis. Work meditatively with these relationships and allow yourself to explore any ideas or correspondences you find.

10) This is an exercise that for most of us will mean working from home. There are many different environments in the world, where plants flourish. They can hang on at the brink of habitable, and frequently the presence of pioneer

plants allows others to follow and colonize. Think about less familiar places where plants grow. You may wish to pick a more exotic location that you cannot visit in person and contemplate the plant life that might inhabit such a region. Again, you can think through the issues raised in other exercises. You can underpin this to good effect with research and then meditate based upon what you have learned. You might want to seek out different habitats to explore the ways plants live in them and the different energies this creates.

Connecting with Creatures

We are more similar to other creatures than might at first seem obvious. We share similar basic life patterns based on growing, feeding, mating and raising young. We are not the only social or communicative creature. Other living things communicate with sound, and body language in ways that are easy enough to recognize and interpret. Social animals have ways of reinforcing those social bonds – grooming being a popular one, they also have hierarchies, ways of sharing resources and resolving tensions non-combatively. Every species is different but we hold much in common and we can recognize familiar things in other creatures.

There is an important balance to strike here. On one side is the risk of over anthropomorphizing, ascribing human traits, beliefs, attitudes or meanings to animal behavior. There are times that won't work or be helpful. They are like us, but there are differences between all species. Equally, we can go too far in the other direction imagining that animals are not at all like us – that they do not feel in a way comparable to us. Emphasizing the differences makes it easier to justify cruel use of animals for our benefit. The more like us we feel they are, the harder we are going to find it to mistreat them.

Working with creatures requires time, patience and

dedication. Winning their trust, acceptance or tolerance takes effort. You can't just walk outside, find a wild creature and expect it to stick around so that you can feel inspired by it. However, creatures are present in our lives and frequently close. Even wild ones will come to tolerate us if we behave in ways they find acceptable. When birds and animals allow us a little closer, or dare to approach us, it's an incredible experience. Even winning the trust of a domesticated animal is something to celebrate and take pride in. Birds can be persuaded to come close for food, especially in lean times. Some will be bold enough to feed from your hand – I've heard stories about sparrows, seen wild starlings do it, and hand fed a wild robin myself. I've heard of people who can get close to badgers even.

Sitting with a plant or contemplating the land is important work, but we don't get much straightforward feedback about how any of it relates to us. Living creatures will respond. At first, they may well just run or fly away. People are so inherently noisy that often the wildlife scarpers long before we even get close. Learning to be quiet, to move slowly and make no sudden movements becomes vitally important. Being able to sit or stand, barely moving, for long periods increases the chances of seeing something wild. Paying a lot of attention to your surroundings is also vital. I've observed Druids in ritual failing to notice rats scampering just beyond the circle, buzzards flying overhead, and other such visitors. Listening, watching for movement and being alert changes what you perceive, and knowing to try in the first place is a big part of that. It's not just a rural issue either. There are plenty of birds, animals and insects in cities too.

If you get it right however, the wildlife stays put, or sometimes even comes to you. It is thrilling when that happens, when you can have a butterfly climb onto your fingers, or watch a mouse in the undergrowth. If the other creature knows you are there and tolerates you, then that is a huge achievement and affords you moments of utter beauty.

As with plant work, you may find there are specific creatures you are especially drawn to working with. I would recommend exploring the main life forms – birds, mammals, insects, fish and reptiles – at least briefly for the sake of completeness and broad insight. However, if you find yourself called to work more deeply with some forms than others, then follow your heart. The following exercises will give you ideas to explore, but there is absolutely no substitute for investing time, and stillness in reaching out to real creatures.

Exercises for Connecting with Creatures

1) Go to a place you are already familiar with, where you have some relationship with the land. Find a quiet and still place to be, and see what creatures become visible to you. Experience their presence and allow yourself to be open to them. Contemplate their relationship with this place and the lives they have – what they eat, how they live, how the seasons affect them and so forth.

2) Pick a creature that is a physical presence in your life and take the time to learn its ways and habits. Without intruding upon it, go where it goes, explore the time of day it favors, consider its food, whether it hunts, or is hunted. How does it drink, and where? If appropriate, you might want to leave food out for it. Working in the space your creature favors (or as close as you can reasonably get without disturbing it) contemplate what it would be like to be the same sort of creature, living that life, in that space. Imagine how your body would feel. Then as with the plant exercises, you can try to reach out to the creature in meditation, to gain a deeper sense of it.

3) To explore creatures in a range of ways, you may wish to

work through the elements in turn, although fire offers less scope here. Think of the creatures of the air and the water, those who go upon the surface of the earth, and those who go beneath it. Contemplate each environment in turn, meditating on how creatures connect to the elements and the spaces available them.

4) If you have a physical relationship with a creature – a family pet or working animal, you may wish to spend time with that animal, contemplating its being and life experiences. You may wish to seek contact with animals through working with them.

5) Hunting and eating would also constitute ways of experiencing and relating to creatures. As a vegetarian, I'm in no position to comment on this in detail, but, if you are eating, or hunting for creatures it makes sense as a Druid to do that in a mindful way, recognizing the spirit and sacredness of the creature just as you would with a plant. The creature can be honored as it is eaten, its life acknowledged and its spirit thanked.

6) As with plant workings, you may wish to seek an animal guide, for inspiration, wisdom or healing. You may want to undertake this through a pathworking, perhaps envisaging walking into a wild space where the creature you seek can be asked, and may come to you.

7) Parts of animals are not so readily or comfortably sourced for working with meditatively. The bones are easiest to work with. Whereas with plants you can take a piece and leave the main plant living, with animals, a body part normally represents a death. Some creatures molt skins, shells and feathers naturally, and these can be found and

worked with. People wishing to work with animal parts tend to use road kill, or creatures whose deaths were not sought for the purposes of gaining such parts. Working with the remains of a dead creature is different from working with part of something that still lives. Not everyone will be comfortable with such explorations. Be guided by your own feelings in this.

8) As animals will not fit in neatly with your meditation plans, you will very likely need to spend some time working from within your home to contemplate different creatures. There are living things in many parts of the world, and so just as you did with plants, you may wish to study and contemplate places and creatures you cannot experience in person.

9) Creatures exist as part of eco-systems and food chains. Contemplate those relationships and the connections that exist between creatures and plants. You may wish to consider what is immediately around you and how it interconnects.

10) Contact with wild creatures happens unexpectedly. If you find yourself in the company of a creature, you may wish to respond there and then with meditation and opening to its presence. This is one of the reasons why it is best not to be dependent on having certain aids in place for meditation. Opportunities to connect come unpredictably and it is good to be able to take them as they happen.

Humans are creatures too. Everything that we learn in relating to other creatures bears applying to human-animals as well. In dealing with each other, we move so fast, bring so much noise, don't listen, make startling movements, don't think enough about natural habitat and natural behavior. Being slow, quiet and watchful with other people allows us to perceive each other in different ways. We devote so much effort to hiding our essential, animal selves, from ourselves and everyone else. Being open to our creature-natures, seeing the nature in other humans and learning to work gently with it, opens us up to new ways of relating.

Connecting with Places

What is the difference between the land, and a place? The two are inexorably connected. Any humanly accessible place is either on land, or connected to it. The only obvious exceptions would be things out at sea – ships and oil rigs particularly. However, the notion of 'place' conveys the idea of an area with a specific identity.

When thinking about human constructions this is fairly straightforward. We have been building, shaping our environments and leaving markers since the dawn of humanity. Sometimes those human places have blended into the landscape such that it is hard to tell where one begins and another ends. Human activity has defined much of the land in the UK, the history of farming, woodland management and urbanization informing so much of what we encounter. Humans have been changing their environment for a long time. Those changes create something that is both a part of the land, and an addition to it. The spirits of places that are have been shaped by humans and have been in ongoing human use are different from places where we have had less influence.

Looking at a building, an earthwork or some other human creation – ancient or modern, it's very easy to see it as a distinct 'place'. With that individuality, comes a sense of distinct character, and spirit. A place in this sense tends to have a name, its own indicator on a map, history and potentially also myth associated with it. The sense of place is a combination of land, construction, use, story, atmosphere and the way in which it moves us.

There are also entirely natural places. Usually these are formed with boundaries that we can perceive, that hold them as distinct and separate. Where one feature of landscape melds into others, we may not perceive distinctions. Consequently, a beach, a spiny of trees, a hilltop, a lake, a dell and so forth are the kinds of natural, bounded features that may strike us as being places, in this sense. Like human constructions, such places often have a distinct character of their own – a combination of land and living things. They too may have history and myth associated with them. We tend to perceive places with stories as being more distinctly individual. It is interesting to ponder to what extent this is an issue of human perception. We respond to things where it is possible to make stories about them – and naming is part of that story-making urge. Large rocks, dramatic waterfalls, hills and other features attract our inclination to name things. Names attract stories. We even do it with fields. However, where there is little variation in the landscape, we can't differentiate with names or with stories.

When we recognize something as being a place, with a unique identity specific to it, are we indeed recognizing a spirit, or are we ascribing human values to non-human things? There is a danger of prioritizing 'places' over areas that it is not so easy to pin down and attach human meanings to. It's easy to make a story around an identifiable place, to create meaning and significance that makes it easier to preserve. That doesn't mean that other, less obviously featured stretches of land are less valuable, just that we don't know how to think about them in constructive ways.

How we designate places as special or important has huge implications. The designating of some land as sacred and other spots as less so affects how we relate to it and what we tolerate having done to it. While recognizing the spirits of place is important in Druidry, how we define 'place' and where we choose not to apply the term, has far-reaching implications for how we relate to the world as a whole.

All places have spirit and all places have history – not all of it human. Maintaining considered relationships with the places we use and inhabit creates a very different experience of them. Some places are easier to love and respect than others. It is important to look at the places we find it hard to relate to, and to explore why – for the sake of self awareness and to seek change in that. The appearance, utility, atmosphere and uses a place is put to will affect how we experience it and feel about it. But if everywhere is sacred, if everywhere is a place and has a spirit, we need to think very differently about spaces that wouldn't normally suggest that to us or seem worthy of care and attention.

Exercises for Connecting with Places

1) Begin with your own home. Take the time to contemplate how your personal space feels, and how you relate to it. What aspects of it please you, and which do not? How does it connect with the land? What else lives in or near it? Simply be open to your immediate surroundings and the energy of it. Does the place have its own spirit? Is that distinctly separate from you?

2) Repeat the above exercise with other places in your life. They needn't be lengthy explorations. A few minutes can be revealing. Try meditating on the nature of a bus stop, or the spirit of your supermarket. Think about the land that has been replaced by buildings. Explore different places, from old to modern; meditate upon their use and atmosphere. Be open to their voices.

3) Contemplate the places you would choose to be in, were

there no practical limitations. Consider how you can bring your own places closer to your ideals.

4) Try to take a few moments to be fully conscious of and open to every place in which you find yourself. Taking a few minutes to experience your surroundings and to honor the energy of the place is important, and means that wherever you are, you are grounded in what you do and open to experience. If you have time to widen that contemplation out, considering the land beneath, the sky above, and the living things sharing the space, then so much the better. Short bursts of this exercise will increase your awareness of your surroundings. More is good, and I aspire to be fully aware and open at all times. It isn't always possible, and sometimes it isn't advisable, but there is much to explore here. Living more consciously, aware of place and other entities, we are connected to so many more aspects of our own lives and selves. We see so much more of what surrounds us, and have scope for understanding so much more. Perception is the beginning of relationship. Developing and sharpening perception at all levels is very much a part of Druidry.

5) When you are in less obviously human-constructed environments, consider how you define 'place'. What is that gives you a sense of a place being special or having its own identity? What kinds of boundaries resonate with you? Groves are traditionally popular with Druids, but what about clusters of trees?

Here are a few thoughts to give you a flavor of what you might experience or appreciate. I'm very drawn to liminal spaces, spots that are not entirely one thing or another. They don't have the most obvious boundaries, and those boundaries can shift – as with beaches, wetlands, river estuaries, anything that is tidally or seasonally affected. Hedgerows and field margins also appeal to me. I like corners and crossroads. One of the things I find it hard to engage with is vast expanses of flat agricultural land. I've never known how to relate to it, but it's also not an environment I spend much time in. I like hidden, secretive places that surprise me – especially little green spaces in urban environments, or where nature is in the process of reclaiming land from us.

Connecting with the Ancestors

Having explored the idea of place, we've already touched somewhat on ancestors. As commented in the section on land, the bones of our ancestors are present in the ground. We live in a world our ancestors did a lot to shape.

Druidry identifies three groups of ancestors – those of blood, place, and tradition. Blood ancestors are the most obvious group – they are the folk from whom we are descended. The grandparents, in countless generations stretching back through time. Ancestors of place are the people who lived on the land before us. We might think of that at a country level, or more locally, as suits us. Sometimes ancestors of blood and place are one of the same, but if they aren't, then you can still recognize those land-ancestors and honor your connection with them. Ancestors of tradition are the only ones we choose for ourselves. They are the folk we consciously follow after in whatever it is we do; parents of craft, belief and action. They might be eco warriors, ancient Druids, modern musicians, or traditional artisans for example. Inspiration draws us to follow them. They could also be our blood ancestors and our ancestors of place.

Ancestry connects us to all living things. We share much of our DNA with the other creatures of this world, and we share ancestors with them too. The further back you go, the more closely related everything is. So while we can think of our ancestors in more immediate and human terms, we can also think of it is a great connecting force. We have many non-human ancestors too.

Our ancestors created us. We carry their genes and their stories. We live with the legacies of what they did and made, we take inspiration from their traditions. Connecting with our ancestors can help us understand ourselves and our own life experiences. It puts our situations into perspective, and often it helps to explain how we got to where we are. Patterns of behavior, attitudes and beliefs may be handed down from one generation to the next. Becoming aware of what we have inherited in this way makes it easier to choose whether or not we wish to carry it forwards.

Very little is new, our ancestors will have experienced many things that compare with our own lives, for although technology may change, the essential human dramas of life, love, sorrow and death, do not. In recognizing that we probably aren't doing anything very new, we gain perspective, and with it the awareness that much can be survived, endured and changed. After all, our ancestors all survived long enough to get us here.

Looking to what the ancestors did may help us find solutions to our own issues. Sometimes we may draw inspiration from the deeds of others, but equally we may look back and realize we want to break the pattern, or cast aside the values that directed our forebears. Our ancestors are not necessarily any wiser than we are, but we have many of them, representing a great deal of collective experience. There is solace to be found in a sense of continuity and connection. Where we connect with non-human entities there is much to learn, but seeking human contact with those who went before us has the potential to be more overtly useful sometimes.

Connecting with the ancestors need not be viewed as a literal speaking with the dead. There are other ways of seeking to understand them. We can explore the stories and lives of our ancestors, both specifically, and more generically through learning relevant history. We can know them through the things they did. Sharing experiences can be a powerful source of insight. Traditional arts and crafts take us closer to our ancestors. Walking where they did, exploring the kinds of clothes they wore, handling things they made or owned, seeing how they lived, exploring historical cooking – there are a great many creative ways in which we can meet our ancestors in a spirit of empathy. It's also possible to look at that which they bequeathed to us. We have our own faces and bodies to consider, buildings, antiques, remnants of ancient cultures. Time spent in a museum can be communion with the ancestors.

We don't have to agree with everything our forebears did. Most modern pagans will have a great many Christian ancestors. Poking around in family trees might reveal the heroes and champions we long for, the enlightened and forward thinking, the granny who was a witch and so on. But just as likely it will show up philanderers, fools, bigots and the like. Most of us would probably find the criminal, the insane, the illegitimate and the otherwise unacceptable amongst our honored dead. We may well not be at ease with more recent ancestors either. It's easy to pin ideals and aspirations to distant predecessors we know nothing of, to explain failings through heritage and to otherwise use the past to justify or explain the present. If we use our ancestry as a reason for inaction, then we misuse that sense of connection. Where our ancestors or the idea of them inspires us and helps us make sense of our own lives, then it's worth exploring.

Exercises for Connecting with the Ancestors

1) Meditate upon your immediate ancestry. Think about the traits in you that come from your recent ancestors, the points of conflict, and the physical inheritance. If you have, or anticipate having descendants then you might

wish to also contemplate their relationship to your family tree, and what of the past is, or will be carried forward in them. See yourself as existing within a tapestry of lives.

2) Contemplate your ancestors of place – the folk who occupied this land before you. You can define 'place' as specifically or broadly as you wish. Think about who they were, how they lived, and what of them remains visible to you. How do they touch your life?

3) Identify your ancestors of tradition – those people from whom you have learned your arts and crafts, or who contributed to those through history. You may not know their names. Consider who has influenced you, who stands as a conceptual parent in your cultural, spiritual or intellectual development.

4) Contemplate your more distant ancestors, the ones you do not know by name and can only guess at. Who do you imagine they were? How might they have lived? What would they make of your life?

5) If there are places or objects that connect you directly to your ancestors of blood, place and tradition, then you might want to work with those in a meditative way, seeking connection to the past through these physical reminders.

6) You might wish to construct a pathworking in which you can imaginatively converse with your ancestors. If you have unresolved issues with the dead, this can be a healing process. You may want to seek their wisdom and insight. Whether you consider answers from them to be coming from your own subconscious or from the actual

spirits of your ancestors is very much up to you to determine, and you may find some meditations suggest one explanation, some another.

7) In time, you too will be an ancestor. Contemplate what forms your ancestry will take. What will you pass on or leave behind? What would you like to be remembered for? What stories might they tell of you after you have gone? This can easily become either very depressing, or total self-indulgence. To look at your own potential legacy, or absence thereof with any clarity, is hard. Recognizing the impact of what we do and how it may outlast us is important. Seeing what we want to leave, and what we need to resolve now can help us better order our own lives.

Connecting with Spirits

Everything material we perceive can be understood as having spirit. However, we may also consider spirit as something more magical and mysterious that lies beyond our perceptions. While understandings of spirit vary from one pagan to the next, some Druids engage with ideas of spirits not only as inherent within the material world, but also as separate and not necessarily corporeal beings. Once we start exploring such spirits, we move entirely away from pragmatic meditation and approaches that are rooted in psychology and personal growth. To contemplate spirits and seek to interact with them is to embrace meditation as a spiritual and magical activity. Anyone who does not perceive the world in this way may wish to skim read the next sections and skip the exercises suggested here. As ever, be guided by your own feelings and beliefs.

As discussed previously, we cannot rationally know if what we experience in meditation is just our imagination or if it taps into other levels of reality, other kinds of truth and relates us in a very real sense to other entities. All of the previous exercises can be used to develop empathy, imagination and insight without any need to believe they are objectively 'real' experiences. My personal belief is that meditation can be any of the things described above, depending on the depth at which one meditates, and the intention of the person making the journey. Some meditations are simple and very much of our own minds and bodies, while others, I feel, blur lines into magic and shamanism. I believe that this will probably manifest in different ways for different people, but can only speak from my own experience.

For the purposes of these exercises, you need to be comfortable with the idea that there are spirits who are not part of consensus reality and that we can use meditation to engage with them. Any of the previous meditations can be approached with the intention of making real connections with actual spirits, as well. What we intend informs what we experience. Discerning meaning is always going to be a personal issue, and in this area of working, that is truer than ever.

Spirits, like anything else might be friendly and benevolent, or might not. Working in meditation, using your own mind as a tool, you are entirely in charge of your own experiences and can remove yourself from them at any time. This is an important point to remember. Deeper meditations can seem beyond our control. Any sense of contact with something other than ourselves, may be disorientating and unnerving. Holding that sense of control is vital. We can step away. We choose how we interpret experiences.

How do we recognize spirit? For me it comes in a feeling of wonder, the numinous sense of touching something that is other. I've lived with small, eccentric presences in my home for many years – they don't interact with me much, but they are present, scuttling about doing their own things. They are part of the place, part of my life. The more open I have been to them, the easier they have become to perceive. I've experienced places that touched me with a profound sense of presence, and others that felt uncomfortably empty. I've had occasional dreams that seemed more real than others. Meditation is the same. Some of it feels wholly internal or the product of my own imagination. On occasion, something far more intense and resonant has occurred. These meditations frequently change or influence me, they shape my sense of self, affect my thinking, alter my ideas, and in doing that, they have an undeniable reality. What has touched me? I don't know. I think of it as spirit, as something aware that is outside of me. I might equally use words like 'deity', 'awen', or 'ancestors'. They do not usually explain who or what they are. Could we explain ourselves to another form of life if asked to? Probably not.

Spirits are like people in that they do not necessarily want anything from us, or have anything for us. Do not assume that spirits you encounter are wise, all-knowing, all-powerful, or even right. They are entities with their own perceptions and intentions. Trying to jump in and get their attention is not unlike pouncing on people in the street – they may be confused by you. Or, think of it in terms of the internet. Typing 'tell me what I should do' on a random message board will not give you a line to the best possible answer you could find anywhere; it will possibly be the opposite. Relationship with spirit, based on sharing, experiencing and interacting is far healthier than trying to get something because you want it. And that includes enlightenment. Each encounter and relationship is different and needs handling on its own terms, but seek them for their own sake, not for what you might gain.

Exercises for Meditating with Spirit

As ever, it begins with perception...

1) We all have moments when a trick of the light, or a coincidental bringing together of random elements creates the impression of a creature. We might see a human shape in leaves whipped up by the wind, for example. The normal response is to disregard these moments as imaginary, or accidental. Be open to such moments, and rather than rejecting them, contemplate them when they come to you, and see where that takes you.

2) If in any of your previous meditations you have had a feeling of otherness, or presence, revisit those meditations with the intention of exploring that sense of spirit.

3) In meditation, ask any spirits that are interested in you to make known how they wish to be worked with. They may reply, or they may not, and you may have to keep asking. If there are answers, they may not come in ways that make immediate sense. This can be a complicated business and it takes time to build insight. Spirits can be very much like people in this regard too, and as unpredictable and fickle as ever people are.

4) You may wish to write a pathworking that enables you to ask benevolent spirits to make themselves known to you.

5) Contemplate how you might seem to a non-human spirit encountering you. What would they understand of you? How would they reach out to you or connect with you?

6) You may wish to reach out meditatively to the spirits and

ask for inspiration. For anyone working creatively, those other forms and ways of being can be a great source of creative energy and ideas. It's hard to read the works of someone like Charles de Lint, or see the art of Brian Froud, without feeling that they have indeed been touched by something other. Much of the most resonant art, music, writing and so forth has a touch of numinous spirit glow to it – hard to express directly in words, but captivating when encountered. Inviting spirits and spirit in a more general sense, to flow through your meditations and your work may lead you in new directions.

Beyond that, I think the journey is inevitably individual because it is about relationship. No amount of exercise or determination will hand it to you on a plate. Finding, recognizing, relating to and being touched by spirit, is a process. You can approach it, you can call out, seek, pay attention, but either something comes, or it doesn't. And if it comes, what follows will be down to you, and any notion of structured exercise becomes meaningless.

Shamanic Meditation

Shamanic journeying is a process by which the spirit of the shaman leaves the body and travels, aided by spirits, into the spirit realms to seek knowledge and the means to heal. I am not a shaman and this is not an area I can talk about with much authority, but its relationship with meditation needs highlighting. Shamanic work is very much about entering a trance state, and there is a belief in literal contact with the spirit world through the trance. There is a fine line, at most, between trance and meditation. Shamanic journeying is facilitated by intense drumming, which gives a feeling of push and immediacy to the experience, but otherwise is not unlike the exercises we've already explored.

At what point does meditation become shamanic trance work? At what point can we confidently say that we are no longer in our own subconscious minds, but engaging with other realities? I have no answer to this. Those who teach generally advocate learning anything bolder and more esoteric from teachers who are available in person. There is much to be said for this in terms of security, wellbeing and support. The reality is that many of us do not have the luxury of suitable and available teachers. Many of us end up learning our craft from a mix of books, trial and error and random inspiration. We probably spend much of our time re-inventing the wheel and making mistakes, we could easily have been spared. All of the human traditions in existence have come into being through human inspiration and exploration. There are advantages to tested and known ways of working, supported by able teachers, but that does not mean these are the only ways.

For some people the journey is a solitary, unguided one, or, there is no human mentor, only the raw experience of spirit as teacher. Some may seek this path by preference, or it may be necessity. How do you find the right teacher when you need them? Paganism offers us no formal structures to turn to, no recognized qualifications or systems. Many teachers become visible by reputation, their work and skill made known by word of mouth. The internet is full of people who will gladly sell you all manner of things and websites loaded with information, much of it incompatible. Having formal teaching by a recognized teacher gives us kudos, and it's a lot easier to be taken seriously with a renowned craftparent behind you. But who teaches the teachers? Is it necessary that we can all trace the roots of our learning back into antiquity? For a seeker who has no wise and trusted mentor to ease the way, there are no simple answers.

Working alone means there are no safeguards, and there is no one to reassure you that what you do is genuine, and not the product of imagination, or insanity. Working alone is a lonely business, fraught with all kinds of difficulties, but if it's what you have, that lone path is often preferable to the kind of distress that comes from not working. The call of spirit and the call to serve are not comfortably ignored. Not everyone is touched in this way – I do not think I am, and that's why it's an area I have not explored in any great detail.

Traditions often come with their own worldview, which may, or may not turn out to fit with your own. The Shamanic worldview I encountered included the idea of an underworld, and a higher world, both inhabited by spirits. The Shaman travels to these, or is carried there by spirit guides. I found the notion of underworld and upper world too straightforward compared to my own convoluted sense of what is. My notion of spirit is of something inherently in this world and part of what we experience, so for me the idea of journeying in this way does not make a great deal of sense, which is simply a comment on me, not on this way of working.

I was once led through an exercise in which, supported by drumming, we descended to the underworld, met the guardian and asked permission to seek a guardian spirit to work with. Others in this meditation group were able to find creature spirits to work with, and had experiences that were, for them, very meaningful. I found myself fruiting from the guardian's tree and dropping to the ground in one form after another, flashed senses of life and death until I was disorientated and exhausted. Sometimes, we try things and they don't work for us.

The principle that meditation takes us into other levels of reality is one I find persuasive. The deeper, wilder meditations take wing in their own way, I find. I would not call it shamanism, although I see parallels. I do not have any name for it. However, once a person starts working deeply, intensely, questing after spirit, insight and inspiration, the path they follow becomes their own, and is an inherently uncertain one. If you find yourself working in this way, there will be nothing but your own wisdom and experience to guide you, unless you are able to seek, and secure a suitable teacher. Genuine and able teachers are not numerous.

Shapeshifting Meditations

During the exercises on connecting with other entities, we touched on the issue of visualizing taking the form of those other beings. Spending time exploring what it might be like to wear a different skin, can bring all kinds of insights. As with the other more magical forms of meditation, this form of work raises questions about its own reality. The more deeply we work with the idea of other skins, the more real that feels. Does some part of us take wing, paw or scale in other forms?

Whether or not you believe that your spirit literally departs from your body, exploring other forms and perspectives is, I think, more interesting than wandering about your immediate environs as yourself. It is possible to visualize yourself leaving your body in order to roam your surroundings in spirit form – but to what end? If you have no particular purpose in mind, it is simply an exercise, but not an inherently spiritual one. Seeking the sense of another form is a way of seeking relationship with other beings. Even if we view this as a purely imagined transformation, it takes us into greater empathy with other beings, which is important work in its own right.

Shapeshifting exercises are difficult to master because there is a great deal of sensory information that you need to hold. It takes time to create the thought form in your head for a different shape and to be able to manage thinking about all the attendant differences and perceptions. Consequently, it is best not to rush with these, take the time to become familiar with each stage before pushing onto the next one. These are meditations that need long stretches of time to explore them, and the peace of not being interrupted. Allow yourself at least twenty minutes for each exercise. You may find you need a lot more time than that.

All the previous meditations we've discussed are easy to surface from, however shapeshifting meditations take time to leave because when they work, you have to mentally readjust to your own form at the end. Make sure you allow yourself the time and energy to do this stage thoroughly. If you find the process of retuning difficult, cut down on the length and frequency of meditation, and spend more time on work that affirms your sense of self. It is well worth balancing shapeshifting meditations with practical, physical activities that reinforce your relationship with your own body.

1) Imagine that you are a tree, roots deep in the soil, branches stretching into the sky. Be aware of your solidity and strength. If you can stand amongst trees to do this, so much the better. Take the time to feel the life in the soil and the way the air acts upon you. Imagine your branches, feel the touch of sunlight. The pace of trees is so much slower than our own, see if you can shift towards it. Stand between the earth and the sky. Be slow about this. Tree forms are in many ways easier to envisage because they don't move. Our bodies readily become trunks, our feet are roots, our hands and arms stretch up as branches. Being a tree is inherently slow, and getting used to the longer time frames needed to explore this is beneficial, in addition to the peaceful states tree shapeshifting meditations bring. Surfacing from this meditation, take the time to re-imagine your own form as it usually is. Because of the stationary nature of tree meditations, I find movement tends to help me ground in myself again, and of the available forms, I find trees by far the easiest, which is why I suggest them first.

2) Pick an animal form that you have worked with before,

and with which you are familiar. Take a few moments to consider the shape of the animal. Imagining yourself into that shape will of course vary depending on what you pick. I find it helps to start at one end of the body and work towards the other, corresponding my own limbs and parts to those of the creature, and working through one anatomical area at a time. Work out the basic structure first, and hold that shape in your head, as your own shape. Be aware of your breathing, and breathe in your creature form. Once you feel settled, start to think about how this skin would feel. Are there feathers, fur, or scales? Are you a lightweight creature or something heavy and muscular? Do you have teeth? A beak? Feel your way into the extremities of this form, explore the edges. Then slowly reverse the process, remembering the shape of your own body and the feel of your own skin. Think your way back into yourself.

3) Once you are comfortable with the above exercise, explore the way in which your creature moves. The more akin to human movement it is, the easier you are likely to find that. You may want to think about how young creatures of your chosen species first move, and use that to help you get started. Again, take the time to carefully return to yourself at the end.

4) When you are confident about moving, meditate on the ways in which your chosen creature lives and visualize yourself moving as it does, living as it does. The longer you spend doing this, the more careful you need to be about returning and grounding.

5) Once you are confident with a specific form, you may wish to explore other possibilities – perhaps to engage

with different elements and environments, or different kinds of creature. These exercises work best when you feel some empathy for the form you wish to take. It is always best to follow your heart.

6) When you are responding to living creatures in their environments, you may wish to meditatively take the same form and follow what they do. With time and practice, it is possible to do this quickly and easily. Responding to living creatures and being led by what you see of them makes the experience more real, and deepens the engagement with the creature in question.

The Sacred Grove Meditation

Back in the pathworkings section, I introduced the concept of a sacred grove meditation – where you envisage yourself being in a grove of trees where you can work specifically as a Druid. I've encountered this practice from a number of sources. The idea of the sacred grove meditation is to develop, within you, a place of calm and spiritual openness that supports and enables your Druidry. The grove you visit in meditation should be the same grove each time, and is your personal, sacred place. Here you can seek advice from guardians, carry out the most private forms of ritual, and connect with the deep roots of Druidry. There are all sorts of reasons why a person might feel drawn to this, and some circumstances in which it will be necessary, but I have my doubts about it.

This, to me, is living room Druidry. It is the Druidry of central heating and safety. The sacred grove in your head is anything you want it to be – dry and sunny are likely features. Dogs will not crap in it. Litter will not be left in it. You will not turn up to find a family having a picnic, kids on mountain bikes or anything else inconvenient to Druid working. It will always be safe, serene and entirely within your control. If your life circumstances mean either that you cannot work outside your home or that you need serenity and control for the time being, then the Sacred Grove meditation, as usually practiced, is probably the version with which to stick.

If you are able-bodied and not in desperate need of security, then I invite you to consider subverting working inside into a far more feral form of Druidic meditation.

Working outside, you are not tied to being in one place. Working continually in the same spot confers the advantages of developing relationship over time, but diversity is good too – so do whatever makes sense to you. Any outside space with a little earth or grass will suffice – your garden is fine. You are picking a place, or places, that will be your sacred grove(s). I had three for some time – a spot in my garden, a clearing in a nearby wood, and the area around a yew tree in another wood. Your 'sacred grove' does not have to be in a wood, but I recommend a spot with trees or plant life if you can find it. Otherwise, work with what you have. The point here is about being real and in your surroundings.

Having the option of sitting is good. Begin by taking the time to walk around the space you wish you use – walking the perimeter is good, or just ambling about until you have enough sense of the space to know where to sit. Be open to the land and its inhabitants, ask permission for what you intend to do and make sure you feel your presence is acceptable. When you are ready, sit in a comfortable position and look around you. Be aware of the plants in your vicinity, the energy of them. If you don't know much about them, you may wish to research them at a later date. Work through a few of the physical meditations to ground and settle yourself. You might want to include one of the protective and calming meditations from the section on physical meditation – envisage the space you have chosen as your safe space, and yourself as protected within it.

You are now in your sacred grove. Rather than going into a pathworking of a grove when you need insight or inspiration, try instead going out to your actual sacred grove space and working in it, and with it. You may find yourself inspired to undertake work for the space. Anything can be a meditation, including litter picking and gardening. Working outside, in a much more real way, you are far more immediately open to experiences not of your imagining. You will experience weather, creatures, disturbances and possibilities that are far more random and productive than always turning inwards to seek the same things within yourself. It is good to look outside of ourselves for inspiration, and meditation should not cut us off from the 'real' world.

You can take any of the previously discussed meditations out to your sacred grove, and try them there. Exercises previously explored indoors will have a significantly different flavor outside. If you keep to the same places, working over many sessions in the same space builds relationship and insight.

At times when you need a reassuring headspace but cannot get to your preferred place for working, you can then visualize your actual sacred grove, rather than having to make one up. For people who find holding the details of visualizations clearly, it can be a great help to have a real place to think about. Contemplating a place where you may have explored your Druidry in more dynamic ways, gives you other points of reference aside from your own immediate emotional state. There can be a great deal of comfort to be found in meditating on a place you know in person, when you cannot be there.

Meditation in Personal Ritual

Later in the book, the topic of meditation in group ritual, will be covered in detail. However, solitary ritual is very different from any kind of shared working. Solitary ritual belongs to the realm of individual spiritual practice, which is why we're considering it first in this section.

Where there are multiple people, speaking aloud is essential to share the experience and enable inspiration to flow. However, when we undertake ritual alone, the pressure for spoken words is much reduced. If we are talking to our deities, or the land, do we need to voice things? This may be a matter of individual taste.

Where there are a group of people sharing ritual, speaking aloud to honor the ancestors, the spirits of place and so forth makes a lot of sense and feels very comfortable. Working alone, saying the same things can seem downright silly. It is of course possible to undertake ritual purely in meditative form. You could go so far as to meditate yourself through a Druid Ritual at a site like Stonehenge, resplendent with any detail you fancy. This would not be the same as doing an actual ritual with real people. Solitary ritual creates considerable opportunity for working with meditation, and blending the two forms. As with all things, there is a balance to seek and strike here. Meditation can add extra depth and soulfulness to ritual working, but it can also tip us into the realm of self-indulgent fantasy and take us out of the reality we inhabit.

For anyone not used to the conventions of Druid ritual, they tend to include some (and occasionally all) of the following elements: honoring the spirits of place, the four elements, and the ancestors, making a call for peace to the four directions, and sharing bread and mead. These actions create a framework that is repeated on the way out of ritual, while the mid-section includes content that honors the season, expresses creativity and shares inspiration. Ritual is a complex art and one that really needs a book on its own. For the purposes of talking about meditation in ritual, I am assuming readers have a degree of familiarity with Druid ritual practice. However, if you don't, and you feel inspired to build private ritual out of meditation practice, then there is nothing to prevent you from so doing. Solitary ritual is inevitably different from gatherings, and there is no 'wrong' way of doing it – as long as it works for you.

Any of the ritual elements described above can be handled through meditation – having worked already with the land, spirits of place, the elements and the ancestors, we've already built familiarity with those energies. These forces and presences can be honored and explored to whatever depth seems appropriate, using meditation in a ritual. Equally, things learned in meditation can be drawn on here for more dynamic expressions when we explore ritual. When undertaking more dynamic rituals, full of words and actions, the central part of a ritual can easily be a pathworking or a visualization appropriate to the season.

In theory, you could sit in your living room, visualize your sacred grove and go through an entire ritual in it, without moving so much as a finger. This is not an activity devoid of merit, and especially useful for planning rituals that will be physically enacted. As with the choice between imagining a sacred grove and being amongst trees, meditative ritual creates the same choices. There is the ease, safety and convenience of working inside your head, versus the hassle and challenge of going somewhere outside. There is also the limitation of your own imagination versus the unexpected gifts of genuine experience. Ritual undertaken in person gives us chance to deepen relationships with places and others.

All of this said, meditation can be used alongside ritual to good effect. You can mix meditation and action in ritual. If you are planning to meditate rituals, I would advocate working in your actual sacred grove rather than just in your head, so that you have a degree of physical experience to reinforce what you do. Even indoors, you can take the time to make a space, create an altar, and interact with things outside yourself. Creativity is an important part of Druidry, and it is well to express that in many ways rather than focusing entirely on the mind.

Below are some ways of meditating ritual. They can be mixed to any degree you like with physical action and spoken word. You can work entirely by meditation, or use meditation to underpin action.

Use your meditation skills to open yourself to the space and listen to its spirit. Then honor the spirits of place, drawing on what you are experiencing. You may not need to say much, but a few spoken words will ground you in the moment and focus your intent.

If you honor the four directions, take time at each to be aware of the element's presence within yourself – earth in the north, air in the east, fire in the south and water in the west. Visualize the element within you as you speak to it.

If you make a call for peace to the four directions contemplate what peace in those parts of the world you turn to might mean. Consider where peace is absent.

When you honor your ancestors, pause first to meditate upon those connections and to be aware of your sense of those who went before you.

Any action undertaken in the central part of a ritual can be explored from a meditative mindset. You might gather natural items from your surroundings and build an altar or mandala, using the action as a physical meditation and the creation as an offering to the spirits. You might use the central part of your ritual to meditate upon a thought form or a subject, or to undertake a pathworking. You might use drumming or chanting.

Ritual undertaken lightly, without thought or care is merely going through the motions or indulging in the pageantry. That of course can be great fun, and it all comes down to what you are doing ritual *for*. Ritual will only ever have the depth and power that we bring to it ourselves. The skills developed through meditation open the way to good ritual, but they do not replace ritual. That said, ritual is not inherently necessary to Druidry either, any more than meditation is. They are ways of reaching out to the mysteries, the energies, the gods. There is nothing wrong with meditating your way through a ritual – especially if you have few other options, but it is different from being 'out there' and it is important to hold that difference in mind.

Grounding and Settling

Returning from a meditation is an important part of the process and you need to allow time for it. The deeper and more intense the meditation, the more time and grounding is called for. The simple, physical meditations are easy to leave, but the more involved we get, the more it takes to shift gears back into the mindset necessary for the rest of life. While using meditation to develop a more conscious way of living is a good thing, there is such a thing as too much meditation. If it takes you away from your life, then you're doing too much. If you have trouble returning to a 'normal' and more dynamic state then reduce the amount of time, or the frequency of meditation.

Generally speaking, meditations, which have you engaging with an external reality, do not cause much trouble. They keep us in touch with our physical selves, and keep us grounded in the world. However, lengthy pathworkings that take you deep inside yourself can create challenges. The more something feels like your spirit has walked in another skin, or another realm, the harder work it is coming back. The good news is that most people do not go straight from a little meditation through to full blown dramatic, shamanic-style experiences. It's a process, and as you learn to go deeper, so too do you learn to make the return journey. Do not push for the bigger, more 'impressive' feats of meditation. Give yourself time. It is not a race or a competition; you are not getting points for duration, endurance, or putting yourself through something that messes with your perceptions the rest of the time. Repetition, mindfulness, use of post-meditation analysis and a placing of meditation within your life are the things that will take you forward. Pushing will not make you go faster, further, or better. Part of the process of meditation calls for letting go of the pace, urgency and achievement orientated nature modern living tends to foster. Learn to be slow. Do not seek to achieve anything.

When you are planning a meditation, remember to plan how you are going to bring yourself back from it. Working alone, you have sole responsibility for this. Asking someone else to intervene takes control of the experience out of your hands and can be very disruptive, so is not a good solution. Plan the walking back out of the scene, whether that's up the stairs, down the hill, or whatever makes sense, to help focus your mind on coming back. Then make sure that you actually do it, and bring yourself back gently, and thoroughly.

When you return from a meditation, don't rush. Give yourself time to adjust and reflect. There's nothing wrong with encountering a little lethargy and disorientation at this point. If you are gentle with yourself for a few minutes, it will pass easily. Do not plan to get up from a long meditation session and leap into action. Instead, allow yourself the time to go over what you've just done. This is the ideal time to write down your thoughts and the process of recording is a good way of clearing your head and getting settled. Take the time to stretch and bend, loosen up your body and be good to yourself. Gentle movement will reacquaint you with your own skin. Something to eat or drink will also help ease you back.

If the process of returning is for some reason traumatic, or leaves you feeling exhausted and seriously disorientated, then that is something to take seriously. Treat it as you would going into shock – you need caffeine, or a hot drink, plenty of sugar, and warmth. I've had this happen to me coming out of intense rituals and very deep meditation, but treating it in the same way as shock works well, and the problem passes.

If you encounter serious difficulty, take the time to ascertain why, and pull back slightly. Do not do any meditation work for a time afterwards – at least a few days – and when you return to meditating, focus on the physical meditations for a while and build back up slowly. If you're having trouble, there will be a reason. Whatever it is, the answer is not to push harder. This is not an area of work where struggling brings any kind of benefit.

Anything can be done to excess and anything done to excess, poses risks. You are responsible for your own experiences and wellbeing.

Chapter Five

Meditation for Groups

There are many good reasons for exploring group meditation. Agreeing to meet and meditate makes it easier to preserve that time, than trying to hold the space for solitary practice. Sharing meditation gives us the chance to share insight, find common meaning and explore the journey in the company of likeminded folk who will probably be sympathetic. There can be much support from this scenario, and it can be very productive. There is also a delightful, social aspect to this, which again appeals to many folks who do not enjoy solitary work. Group meditations can be a good addition to the life of a community – especially for groves and moots where the shared spiritual framework can be explored and reinforced in meditative work.

When I first started exploring group meditation, I did so because the people around me were interested in it. Although I wasn't hugely experienced, I had been to a few workshops, learned techniques alongside studying Tai-Chi and picked up other ideas from an assortment of magazines and personal experimentation. I did not have the necessary experience to run a meditation group as far as I knew. However, there was no one any better qualified available, and there were people who wanted to explore.

This is the choice that faces many people who undertake to run moots, groves, rituals, drumming circles, meditation groups, bardic chairs and anything else creative and inspiring. When we start, we have little idea of what to do or how to do it. The nearest teacher may well be nothing like near enough, or we may be breaking new ground, where there is no one else to show us how to proceed. However, if we limit ourselves to the things we can safely learn from experienced others, our scope is sorely limited. Often, what is necessary, is for some enthusiastic, under informed and radically inspired person to jump in and try anyway. It's a process laden with risk and full of opportunities to mess up. At the same time, in taking that risk we open door after door to new possibility.

One of the first things I learned is that you do not need to be an expert to run something. If you have a group of co-operative, enthusiastic people, and someone willing to take the helm, then the process of learning can be a shared one. There need be no authority. Even if the person nominally leading knows more than the rest, they will likely find it a learning process anyway. There is always more to discover. Facing the questions and unexpected directions others take will cast your experiences in a new light and make you think in unfamiliar ways. To be a teacher is to be a student. If you aren't learning as you teach, you're missing out.

When I started leading meditation groups, I hunted around for a likely looking book that would tell me how to do it. I didn't find one. There wasn't anything much I found on the Druid side either about the role of meditation in spiritual practice. To a large extent, my aim in this book is to write the material I could have done with a decade ago. Reading it will not qualify a person to run group meditations, but it will give you plenty to play with and some idea of what might happen along the way. The only thing that qualifies you, is doing it.

Creating and Structuring the Group

There are a great many things to consider when setting up a meditation group. Who is going to take part, and where are you doing it, are the most important issues to begin with. If you have a moot, grove or other established group and are drawing from that, then the question of 'who?' is easily tackled. If you don't, then the issue of 'where?' may need contemplating alongside this. People who already know each other and already meet up probably have spaces they can use, or are comfortable enough to gather in each other's living rooms. If you're going to advertise to strangers or include people you barely know, a suitable space is critical. The back room of a New Age shop may suffice, but a quiet room behind a pub probably won't. Quiet and privacy are essential, especially in the delicate early stages when people are easily put off. Once you get into hired halls, you have the issue of who pays the bills and takes financial responsibility. Are you going to charge people, or ask for donations? What happens if you can't cover costs? Are you going to need insurance? It becomes a complex business with legal implications. If this is all unfamiliar territory, I would strongly recommend starting small, and in the company of people you already know and trust. Meditating can be a very emotionally exposed thing to do in a group.

From experience, I would recommend having at least four people in your group, with a starting maximum of eight or nine. If there are too few people, sharing may feel more exposed. It can become too intense. A slightly larger group makes more space for a variety of experiences and creates a better atmosphere. The more people there are however, the more organizing you need to do and the harder it is to hold the right atmosphere. If you go beyond ten people, managing the group becomes hard work and the group will not be as close. When you have more experience running things, larger groups become more feasible, but there is much to be said for intimacy. There is also, once again, the issue of space. You need enough room that everyone can sit comfortably. It's much easier to find a room big enough for eight than sixteen. The more people there are, the more scope there is for personality clashes, or not being able to find dates everyone can do. Again, this creates work and potential complications.

It is important to have a structure, and clarity about how it all works, and to stick with it. Figure out beforehand how you want things to happen, and make sure everyone knows. Democracy is a nice idea, but it doesn't suit situations where responsibility isn't evenly distributed. In practice, the person or persons who lead meditations will be in charge, and need to be in order to have the group functioning well. If someone else owns the space being used, then the authority and responsibility of the space-owner also needs taking into account. People who are not contributing to making it go, should not be allowed to dictate terms. When you do things as a volunteer, it is very important to retain control. If people feel that you owe them, or that they are 'entitled' to your time and energy, some of them will abuse this feeling of power.

Work out at the outset what the intended frequency of meetings is, and where they will be held, who has the right to change that under what circumstances, who is invited, and who is allowed to invite other people. Make these things very clear and do not change them without making the planned change very clear before implementation. In my experience, it's best to fix dates or frequencies and then just have people turn up or not as they are able. Trying to accommodate other people's needs for flexibility can compromise the project and makes a great deal of work. Not having clarity about who has the power to issue invitations can cause confusion and offence. Be careful about who you invite, or allow others to invite on your behalf. Meditation work is sensitive, personal stuff, and the wrong person can make everyone uncomfortable. Make sure you keep a right to veto, and a right to ask people not to come back if they don't fit in.

You may need to consider whether you will include children. Some people may not be able to attend unless their children do too. Some younger people may wish to participate. Other people find any kind of thoughtful work harder if there are children present and may be uncomfortable about openly sharing their experiences in a group with younger folk. Take into account the age and nature of the young person. If they are not inherently disruptive, you can consider them as long as they have parental support. Adults are just as capable of being disruptive as children and teens. It is worth considering how you might handle such issues before they occur.

If you are offering to run a meditation group for others, then I would recommend running it as a benevolent dictatorship. It can only be a democratic group if responsibility is truly shared. If there is an inequality of responsibility, then an equality of power is neither fair nor workable. If you are giving freely of your time, energy and creativity, then you need to be able to do that on your own terms, for it to be sustainable. Running a meditation group is demanding, takes a lot of energy, creativity, organizing power and concentration. You may not be seeking money for this, but you should expect respect and co-operation. Do not tolerate anyone who thinks that you owe them, or that they have a right to make demands upon you as a consequence of what you are giving.

At the same time, in stepping up to run a group you are taking some responsibility for the emotional wellbeing of your people while they are in your sessions. They remain in charge of their own experiences, but will be trusting you to guide them well and responsibly, and to support them if things become complicated. You will not know the fears, wounds and nightmares of each person you work with, and may well stumble on unexpected triggers. While you are not responsible for an unintended trigger, you are responsible for helping deal with the consequences. There will be more on this later in the chapter.

Where and When to Meditate
This may well be decided for you by the nature of the group you are working with, or the kinds of resources you have available. Here are some points to consider. Your choice of time and place may well influence who is able to attend and the kind of work you are able to do. You don't need much to make a space suitable

for meditation, but a wrong space, that feels insecure, is disrupted, or physically unsuitable will limit you.

- What frequency of meetings can you sustain? Meet too often and you may run out of enthusiasm and ideas, meet too infrequently and you won't hold any group identity or sense of community. An irregular gathering takes more organizing than one happening at set intervals, and people are more likely to forget if it isn't fixed.
- Do you want to meet outdoors? Many of the physical meditations work best outside, and if you wish to explore the communing exercises then you need to be out of doors for best effect. Is your group equally able to get around? What will you do in the event of the weather being unsuitable?
- Are you going to hire a space? How are you going to handle the financial implications, if so?
- Are you going to advertise the event, and if so, where? (I would personally recommend against doing so if you are new to this. Stick with people you know and folks recommended by others.)
- How big a space do you actually need?
- What other resources do you require? If you are outside, you may want to think about access to shelter, toilets and refreshments. Indoors you will need those things too. Consider how people will get to your venue.
- What time of day are you meeting? Consider your own convenience and the needs of your group. Meditating at night has a different feel to working in daylight. Do you need to vary meeting times according to the intended meditation?

Other Guidelines
Do not permit the use of alcohol, tobacco or any other non-

medical drugs in your meditation sessions. You will not be able to maintain the right atmosphere if people are indulging in substances, nor can you be held responsible for their wellbeing. It is also worth avoiding caffeine whilst meditating.

Require all those attending to treat each other with respect. People need to be able to speak of their experiences in a safe, supportive environment. If a participant is rude, dismissive or otherwise demoralizing, you will need to stop them immediately and take them off privately to tackle the issue. Anyone who cannot respect the experiences of others, should not be included again.

Often very private things can emerge in the context of meditation. If something is offered that seems private, ask the person whether this is something they need the others to respect as a secret.

Set a clear start time, allow some time for people to settle, and do not indulge people who are habitually late. Also set an intended time for finishing and try to keep to it – this is essential if you are hiring. It's also important to define the time you are giving, and to be able to step away when you are done.

Make sure all technological devices are turned off throughout the session.

Creating the Setting
While in private meditations, dependence on incense and music is not optimal, group meditations create different requirements. You have a number of people who need to shift from their regular ways of being into quieter, more meditative states. However, groups of people readily fall into chat and gossip. They can easily reinforce each other's usual ways of being, making it hard to shift

mindset for the meditation. One person has considerable control over their own thought processes, but groups can be shaped or thrown very easily, especially if you have one or two dominant or disruptive folk in the mix. People who are nervous or unsure of what to do are more likely to flap, or chat. Creating the space is a way of giving people a sense of who and how they need to be – and folk will respond to these cues. Making sure the meditation session doesn't become a chatty 'did you see that thing on TV the other night?' session, requires attention. If people come into a space with soft lighting, incense, and floaty music, then they are more likely to change mindset.

Candles are lovely to use, so long as you can place them safely and they won't be a problem with people moving about. Ambient music can be good, but lots of stereos create a surprising amount of light, so check for this and make sure one source of 'ambience' does not conflict with the others. Make sure that you have easy access to the controls and don't have to disturb anyone to sort out lights or music. Check beforehand that no one has allergies or asthma that would make incense use a problem. You may also want to be alert to people with phobias – fears of the dark and claustrophobia can be accidentally triggered in meditation sessions. I only found this out after I'd plunged a group into total darkness, which was not ideal.

The space you are using will dictate the kinds of things you can do to create an atmosphere. In hired spaces, you may not be able to use burning materials. You may also be limited in terms of managing light levels. Check in advance to see what you can do to create a good atmosphere in your chosen space. However, there are other tools at your disposal, and you can use other things to create a feeling of otherness and magical possibility if needs be. You may need to bring in objects, cushions or throws to create the space. Setting up an altar, bringing in plants, flowers, wood and leaves will change the feel of the most banal hired hall. Colorful drapes and floor cushions help create a relaxed atmosphere. If you can't do anything else, encourage people to remove their shoes, as this takes them away from 'normal' and does aid relaxation. Avoid having people sat on hard chairs around tables, as this feels too much like a formal work scenario.

If you are working outside, then creating a sense of space is, in some ways, harder. Working in a natural environment is great for many things, and gives you inherent beauty. If you pick your spot well, peace will also be a feature. The physical meditations do not require the same still peacefulness as more cerebral work, but you still need those attending to be focused on the task in hand, not on swapping news. You are limited in terms of the props you can usefully use, and it makes sense not to take electronic music into a natural space. Getting people to listen to the sounds of nature will be good for them, but it's getting them to be quiet enough to listen in the first place that is most often the challenge.

Make sure you are first on the scene. If you are sitting, or standing serenely when others arrive, and greet them quietly, you can help them transition into an appropriate mindset. Carrying small bells or some other softly percussive thing may help you draw attention without having to raise your voice. You might want to play music, if you are a musician, or invite someone who is – the soft tones of harp or flute are magical when working outside. Sometimes the best way to get a group to become quiet and focused is to do it yourself, and wait for them to grasp the idea. Be still, silent and patient. Sit and wait for them. When they are ready, they will find their own silence and join you. I've spent nights on hills when it took hours for this to happen, but when the silence finally came, it was profound indeed. If you don't have that kind of time, then bring people into the right space by speaking softly – whisper to them. Encourage them to listen to the sounds of nature, to be aware of the place they are in, and to enter into its peacefulness.

More than any other aspect, it is you as the leader of the meditation who creates the atmosphere. If you are calm, softly spoken and moving gently then you can draw others into that. Equally, if you are loud, gossipy or flapping your arms about at the outset, the chances of creating a good atmosphere are slim. Before embarking on group meditation, take some time for yourself. Make sure you are centered and ready. Do a few breathing exercises, and make sure your own thoughts are clear. Don't get drawn into talking about how you are, or how your day went – save that for later. It's also important not to dwell on any nervousness you experience. Focus on being calm, open and peaceful. All else will flow easily from this.

You have practiced, and planned. You know what you intend to do (planning suggestions are below), and how you will do it. You are not there to answer questions, solve problems or heal wounds. You are simply creating and holding the space that enables others to do their own work. You can encourage them, listen, support and cheer, as that is part of making a good space. You can take care of the physical space and make sure it is suitable for the work intended. And then the only thing to do is let go, and let it happen.

Structuring Group Meditation

People concentrate best if they aren't required to be too focused for too long. When people are new to meditating, their ability to hold a meditative state is limited. It is best to start with short bursts and work people up to longer sessions. Having one member of your group fidgeting is enough to throw everyone off. I found it works best to do a number of short exercises within a session – aiming to have the whole event last no longer than an hour. This means there is time between each activity to discuss it, opportunity for toilet breaks, and chances to move and stretch. Taking breaks is important to keep people fresh, but you need to make sure the time is not overtaken by chatty trivia where the atmosphere is lost.

This is the structure for group meditation that I settled on – it's simple and flexible. More experienced groups may wish to include more things, but there's a lot to be said for keeping it straightforward. Also, the longer a session is, the more demanding it is to run. Running a meditation session is not remotely like meditating, and can be mentally exhausting if you push on for too long. As an organizer you need not only to remember the plan and enact it, but also to pay attention to how everyone is doing, ready to change things if they aren't working. This is something you learn by doing. Even when people are trying to seem serene and thoughtful, they will have 'tells' if something else is going on. Shifts in breathing and posture can flag up if someone is struggling, unhappy, unable to focus or otherwise having a hard time. There may be individual reasons for this, but if the whole group are showing signs, it means you need to rethink! Every person and every group are different, so see what works and develop your strategy accordingly. In the meantime, here is a structure to play with.

Give people time to settle after arrival. Offer water, fruit juice and so forth to drink and make sure anyone who needs the toilet has been! Turn off all phones and other devices. Encourage people to be quiet at this stage, talk softly, play soft music etc.

Opening – A ten-minute meditation to get people relaxed and settled. Any of the stationary meditations for the body work well for this section, for example breathing exercises, joint opening visualizations. Vary which ones you use from one session to the next.

Allow people a few minutes to properly surface from this and to talk quietly, commenting if they need to on the meditation. Do not allow a 'chat' session to develop.

A deep contemplation session – Give people a choice of natural objects, draw on a pack of divination cards, invite people to bring items – you can vary this a great deal. Allow people time to contemplate their item and then report back. If you are working outside, this is a good time to send people off, as an alternative, for more active physical meditations. Cloud watching, gazing into leaves, or looking at the ground from close to can all be effective. Fifteen minutes or so is good for this. Give people time to report back afterwards, sharing impressions and insight.

Allow a short break for topping up drinks, visiting the toilet, moving and stretching if the previous exercise was sedentary.

Undertake a pathworking, or other intense visualization exercise. Allow twenty minutes for this. Afterwards, give people time to report on their experiences if they wish to share them. Aim to make the content of these different every time. You can revisit similar themes and settings, but make sure people always have something new to play with.

Sharing food and drinks – it's fine to move into caffeinated beverages again at this point, or small quantities of alcohol. Give people time to ground, and to socialize. Make sure you are able to say 'enough' and bring the gathering to a close, or leave it. The concentration called for in organizing is considerable. Each session will afford insights and give you a lot to think over. You may well find yourself tired and in need of the space to mull over how the gathering went.

Guided Meditations for Groups

The difference between meditation and guided meditation is that with the latter, someone is telling you what to do as you do it. For the purposes of this section, I'll assume that you are the person who will be guiding. When a person leads a meditation, they take responsibility for presenting it and making it hang together. They probably also take responsibility for constructing it. Managing the timing for the benefit of participants is the job of the guide. The process of guiding a meditation is entirely different from meditating – it puts you outside the experience, watching over other people and helping them through the experience. Rather than exploring your own ideas, you are facilitating other people and your attention must be focused on them. You may find that ideas occur to you as you speak the meditation – which it fine – but it is vital not to be distracted by your own thoughts from the work of guiding. I found the best way through this was to explore the meditations alone first, and then share them with others.

Meditating alone, you can learn the gist of the meditation and work it from memory, or you can work from a recording of your own voice. As you know yourself, this is not difficult to organize. When you lead a meditating group, the process becomes significantly more complex. Firstly, all content needs to be addressed to 'you' and needs to make sense regardless of the age, gender or other variants between participants. All meditations need to be voiced in the moment. In low lighting, reading from a sheet is not easy. The rustling of paper or stumbling over a word can throw the meditators. For best effect, you need to have the meditation in your head – not necessarily learned by rote, but so that you can produce the key points confidently and in the right order. This may take practice.

When you voice the meditation, your speech needs to be slow and measured, and above all else, clear. You need to keep the volume down whilst making sure that everyone can hear you. Watching the meditators will guide you in this. If everyone looks relaxed and happy, then all is well. Frowns will clue you in to instructions that came too fast or weren't clear enough. Repeating things is fine. You need to lead the group in slowly, focusing them on their breathing and the process of relaxing before you take them into the detail of the meditation. Leave plenty of gaps. When you pause, your group has the time to think for themselves and to work through their own experiences. If you rush, they won't have time to make anything of your pathworking.

Everyone works at a different pace. Judging the length of pauses required is a critical skill for making the meditation effective. The larger your group, the harder this is to manage. Watching the faces of your group, you can get a sense of how they are doing. If people are waiting for you to continue, they will probably fidget in small ways. Everyone finishes at different times, so you will have to make a best guess at the optimal time to move everyone on. Don't assume they have completed whatever task you set them. 'Wherever you are now, I want you to ...' is the kind of approach you need to move them along without jolting them. You have to be paying attention to your group all the time to judge the timing and watching for people who are struggling in any way. The more able you are to judge where the meditators are and what they might need, the better the session will be. This takes a great deal of attention and concentration but makes all the difference. Finding the right pace for the group will radically improve their experiences. Do not assume that your natural pace will be the same as anyone else's.

Consider the pace people go at when designing the meditations. You need to avoid scenarios where people need to finish a specific thing before they can move on. If, for example, you ask folk to wander a wood and find a key that will take them through a door and you say 'now you unlock the door,' if they haven't found the key yet, the reality of the meditation will break down for them. There will always be someone who cannot find the key, or instead finds a talking mushroom, or their grandmother. Be certain that however simple your plan, someone will subvert it. If, instead you move them on by telling them 'you have found the key' then if they haven't found it before, this will probably trigger them to do so, and then you can enter the next stage. The difference is small, but critical.

When it comes to sharing experiences, you need to lead this

in an active way, creating a space in which people feel able to speak. Either ask if anyone wishes to comment and see who speaks up, or makes eye contact, or simply go round the group in turn and ask each member if they wish to comment. Make sure everyone has the chance to speak. No experience is invalid, no matter how strange it may seem to anyone else. If someone is reluctant to speak, reassure them that it is fine not to feed back. No one should feel pressured or uncomfortable at this stage. If people are slow to speak, you can offer your own experiences with the meditation – by sharing something personal of your own you can make it easier for others to open up.

The pathworking narratives previously described in this book work just as well for groups as it for individuals, but will likely require some changes in approach. As with other guided meditations, you need to voice the guidance, clearly, leading people through the narrative you have created for them. The writing process will be much the same, as for solitary workings, but you need to avoid excessively personal elements. Take into account the people you are working with. Contexts, symbols and references need to make sense to your participants, so try to accommodate them as far as your insight permits. Avoid anything obscure – you don't want to alienate participants or make them feel foolish.

When it comes to presenting the pathworking, then timing becomes much more of an issue than it is for solitary work. When you begin the pathworking it is important to give your group time to settle into the notion of pathworking. Describing a physical walk into the setting is good for this. Start with something easy and familiar – imagine you are walking down a staircase, along a path or through a forest. Make it easy to imagine. If you want to introduce less familiar elements, do so slowly. In this opening stage, make sure you offer a range of details – what they can see and hear, perhaps smell as well. Make it vivid and engaging and give them time to settle.

Once you enter the stages where you want your meditators to explore with their own imaginations, you have to consider the timing. Your own time requirements for exploring will, at first, be the only guideline you have for guessing what other people may need. However, everyone is different and as observed before, the only way to gain any sense is through watching. You want to be aiming for fifteen to twenty minutes for the overall pathworking – especially for the first few sessions, so try to keep track of time. Allow meditators a few minutes to explore simpler ideas, a little longer for more complex ideas and then move them on.

The process of moving your group on through the scenario requires gentle direction – people can go off at all sorts of tangents within the pathworking, so you need to round them all up without jolting them too much. If you've given them a task, or a thing to get through, you need to be able to take them on from there.

For example, if you look at the bridge crossing scenario in one of the sample pathworkings, you will see that there is a bridge to cross with a source of fear upon it. This is simple for one person, but in a group, people will deal with that at different times and some could potentially be stuck. You can't assume everyone is across the bridge in the time frame you choose. Nor will it be entirely clear when everyone has crossed. You might, when setting up the bridge scenario, ask folk to raise a hand when they are across, and this may solve the problem. However, if someone can't overcome their fear and cross, you need to move them on or they are going to feel uncomfortable. Asserting 'even if it didn't seem like you were getting anywhere, you find you have made it across the bridge' is probably enough to resolve it for them. When you set up a scenario that people may not be able to work through, make sure you have a way out of it for them.

If someone is visibly distressed, but opts to stay in the

meditation, then allow them the space to do that but make sure they feel supported afterwards. If anyone breaks with the meditation and opens their eyes, make sure they know you are aware of what's happened, but if you can manage it, don't stop the flow of the meditation for others. If someone has removed themselves from the scenario you have created, allow them the space to do that, respect their choice, hear them if they want to speak about it, and respect their silence if they need to hold it. If you run a scenario that appears to be throwing a large number of your group, then soften it, and bring them all back. This is unlikely to happen, but it's worth being prepared for such eventualities.

At the end of the meditation, you need to lead people through their return carefully. Take time over this. Talk them along a path that resembles the way in, as this is by far the easiest. Encourage them to return to their bodies, to awareness of themselves as they are in this place and in this moment. Watch your group. As people return to themselves, they will change posture, shift in their seats, stretch and change breathing patterns. You need to be watchful for people who are not returning easily. Most of the time, most people will be fine. If anyone seems to be struggling, speak to them by name and keep talking to them until they open their eyes. Some people need more time and support on occasion. Keep calm, be patient, keep talking calmly and you will be able to return them.

Sharing Experiences
Getting people to share their experiences of the pathworking will give you valuable insight into what worked and didn't. No pathworking ever works perfectly for everyone. Different people will respond to different settings and challenges, and you will not be able to please everyone totally all the time. However, seeing what works best for people, means you can fine-tune your narratives and presentation style. Allow yourself the space to

learn without feeling as if you need to please everyone all the time. I found that my groups responded best to natural settings, and that anything urban or man-made didn't work. However, I have heard of other groups who were fine with more artificial scenarios. I explored soft and mythic fantasy, but I've never worked with a science fiction setting or anything overtly 'off world' – but some groups of people might respond well to this. Your own enthusiasm must guide you here, but listen to the people you are working with and find out what inspired them too, as you will learn from this.

As previously discussed, meditations can be interpreted and analyzed in the same way as dreams. When it comes to sharing experiences of group meditation, this is an issue to tackle carefully. Everyone's inner landscapes and symbolic languages are different. Things that may be profoundly meaningful for one person may make no sense for another. It is important not to assume anything about the meaning of anyone else's experiences, and, as the one holding the group together, it is important to make sure that no one else attempts to push interpretations onto others either. Sharing ideas is fine, offering possibilities can be helpful, but understanding the meditation must remain in the control of each individual and no one should feel pressured into accepting someone else's interpretation.

If someone is struggling to make sense of an experience, encourage them to consider how it made them feel, what associations it had for them, what it makes them think of. Not everything will lead to clarity and insight, so if they can't make sense of it, reassure them that the uncertainty is not a problem. Not everything has deeper significance, and not all significances show themselves immediately to us. Sometimes things become clearer with time.

Frequently the content of meditations is personal. Sometimes it can be deeply suggestive of all manner of things. In this, meditations are like dreams. Sometimes people will be speaking of things drawn from real experience, and sometimes they won't. If you have any concerns about something an individual says, explore it with them gently, and in private. You are not responsible for how anyone else thinks or feels, so unless they bring an issue to you, do not feel under any obligation to raise it.

Be prepared for all kinds of emotional responses, including tears and expressions of anger. Do not take it personally. Give people the space to express and share. If they feel supported and know they are being heard, then they will feel secure. Whether or not they explain is up to them. Meditation is not about making people open up to each other. Sharing is a tool that can be helpful, but if people don't want to explain, they don't need to.

Usually how a person feels after the meditation is the most important thing. Even if they can make no sense of what they've done, if they feel relaxed, then it's been worthwhile. Meaning is not always necessary or helpful. People may not choose to be honest, either, if their meditation was too personal, or the interpretations that occur to them are uncomfortable. Never push or challenge even if you disagree with what you are hearing. That's not your job, and the truth of what anyone experiences is entirely their own.

Challenges and Problems

As with any group, meditation groups can experience issues with personality clashes, people who can't fit in with proposed time scales and so forth. Running a group means taking responsibility for fielding these issues. Maintaining the focus and intention of the group is the priority to consider in figuring out how to handle any such problems. The other important factor to take into account is your own needs. Look at the energy required to manage the group. If someone is taking too much attention or causing too much difficulty, the entire project may become unsustainable. Sometimes, individuals can be surprisingly needy and because you have set yourself up as 'in charge' they may expect you to be mother, father, nursemaid, personal life coach, cheer leader, agony aunt and magical fix everything person. This is not your job, but if you are inspired to serve, then ignoring the difficulties presented by another can be hard. Community, after all, depends upon sharing and mutual support. Where all you are being asked to do is hear, witness and make encouraging noises, it won't be too much of a strain. The people to watch out for are the ones who want you to make their decisions for them, who keep presenting with the same problems and refusing to tackle them, or who want to run the group through you and feel entitled to make demands. If anyone indicates a feeling that you owe them something, or that you are obliged to do what they want, these are not people you want to work with.

Identifying and dealing with troublemakers is hard, and uncomfortable. I've been there more than once and cannot claim it gets any easier with practice. We want to believe that the folk we work with are all going to be lovely, reasonable, dedicated and reinforcing what we do. Most of them will be, but it only takes one who isn't to make the work miserable and excessively demanding. Even if it feels very uncomfortable to do so, it is necessary to protect yourself from this kind of leeching. If someone is taking from you, do not work with them.

Everything we do is a process, a chance to learn. There will be mistakes. Some of them will be yours. Meditation is a very personal activity that can bring all kinds of unmanageable emotions to the fore. You run the risk of making people uncomfortable or challenging them in ways they cannot cope with. To do anything is to take risk. Think carefully about how you handle your own mistakes. Make sure you support people if you put them in awkward positions. Be clear that they hold absolute responsibility for what they experience and remind them of how to step away if a meditation isn't working for them. Learn when things go wrong, and give yourself permission to try again. If we set out with the assumption that we must be perfect in all things, it's very difficult to get anything done or break new ground. There will be surprises and uncertainties to throw you. Leading, learning and doing the best you can is a process, a journey in its own right. Try to be gentle with your own mistakes whilst avoiding repeating them.

Groups tend to eventually fail from natural causes – if they have served their purpose, if people choose to move on for their own reasons, or if you no longer have the energy or inspiration for the work. All groups and activities have their seasons, and recognizing that a thing is past, is an important skill. There is no dishonor in reaching the natural end of a thing. When the time comes to move on, be clear, and let go.

Chapter Six

Meditation for Ritual

Meditation can be a great addition to group ritual. While I've touched on solitary ritual before, there isn't the space in this book to fully explore the issues of ritual work and organizing ritual groups. The things previously explored that are true of managing groups generally will also apply to ritual settings. Below are some issues that I think are especially relevant when considering the use of meditation in group ritual. For this chapter I am going to assume that you have an existing ritual group and are considering using meditation as part of ritual. Druid ritual for groups should be a much more complex experience than just the meditation aspect, so this is not any kind of stand-alone guide for running group rituals. If you do not have a ritual group or ritual experience to draw upon, then you might be able to improvise based on this chapter, but I can't promise it will be sufficient.

There are also private ways of working with meditation in group ritual settings, which I will also explore in this chapter. Therefore, if you aren't leading a group, but are able to attend something, you may find useful ways of working from this.

Equally, you don't have to be the person running a ritual group to offer to run a meditation within it. If you have a relationship with a group already, then asking to explore this is a good way to go. People who organize rituals are frequently glad of offers of input from others. However, if you do not hold full responsibility for the group, expect to talk in advance about what you mean to do – so that it can be fitted effectively into the overall shape of the ritual, and so that those with responsibility feel confident that your intentions will suit the gathering. Expect to have to earn trust.

What is the purpose of using meditation in ritual? Firstly, it's something most people will easily be able to engage with. In group ritual, giving people scope to be more than just an audience, is very important. Secondly, it is a way of making the ritual experience deeper and more meaningful, because it encourages people to contemplate. The choice of what kind of meditation to use must be led by the kind of ritual you have. When you know exactly who will be present, and what they can cope with, you have the freedom to tailor meditations very specifically. With open rituals, when you won't know numbers much less capabilities, it's important to pick exercises that everyone can do – even children. I've had people opt to sit out of guided meditations in open rituals because they felt uncom-fortable – so be prepared for that eventuality. Location may also influence your choice of meditation, as discussed in the previous section.

Private Meditation in Group Ritual

If you are exploring group ritual, then regardless of how the group is structured and led, there is nothing to stop you from using your meditative skills consciously within the ritual setting. This can be an entirely private undertaking, and in many ways, if you are working alone in a group context, keeping that to yourself will make it easier for you to work. Having other people pay a lot of attention to what you are doing, or not doing, will be a distraction and will likely only make you, and them, uncom-fortable. Avoid situations where anyone might feel you are trying to do some kind of spiritual one-upmanship. Ritual settings are not a contest to see who can be the most 'druidy' and any incli-nation that way must be avoided. I'm sure we all have moments of wanting others to see, recognize and applaud us for being *such* good Druids, but feeling it and acting on the impulse are two very different things. After all, we have no idea what work others are quietly doing, unbeknownst to us. Everyone's experience in ritual is unique, and no one experience is necessarily better or worse than another. What we get depends a great deal on what we do and how we relate to it. A meditative approach is simply a tool for shaping our own experiences.

Below is an exploration of how and where we might privately meditate during a group ritual. It follows the Druid ritual form I am most used to, but not all groups will work in the same way. However, this should be adaptable – leave out elements that are irrelevant, and use the gist of it to help you tackle anything I've not included. This is not a definitive guide to meditating privately during public ritual, just a place from which to start. You can build individual practice based on your own needs and experiencing, innovating as you go. It's not necessary to approach all elements of ritual in a meditative way. Be guided by the limits of your concentration, and consider what else you need within the ritual context. If there are other ways to participate, embrace them, and do not ignore the important social function of group ritual either.

Entering the ritual space, take time to attune yourself to it. You might want to take a slow, meditative walk around the perimeter. Contemplating the land and the other beings present in the ritual space – including other participants, is something you can explore before the ritual begins. Being more familiar with the ritual space will affect how you experience the ritual itself, and will probably give you a greater sense of involvement. If you do nothing else meditatively in group ritual, do this, because it will move you into a good head-space for ritual and give you a relationship with the place you are using that will ground every-thing you then do.

When the circle forms, if you are working with a tightly cast circle of protection, you may want to visualize that. Often people casting circles describe their intent and you can contemplate that as they go. Where circles are looser – as is often the case in open Druid ritual, be conscious of the circle of people, the flow of energy, the sense of temporary temple and community. Give your full and focused attention to what is happening and let the words of whoever is leading guide you as though you were in a guided meditation.

I like to honor Spirits of place right of the beginning of ritual, although sometimes others do this a lot later on. Your initial time dedicated to the place will make it easier for you to engage deeply, and knowingly at this point. If you have taken the time to recognize the spirits of place already, it is easier to give this time to honoring them and being open to their influences.

If the group honors the three worlds, or the four directions, then again as people speak on this, you can use their words to guide your meditations. You can imagine the elements within your body or contemplate their presence in the circle. If a call for peace is made, you can use that time to meditate on peace. Equally, if the ancestors are honored, you can use the words to guide a few moments of meditation on your own ancestry.

Any ritual action can be deepened with meditative contemplation. Rituals may well feature drumming, chanting and dancing, or creative expressions, which you can approach in your own way. I find with ritual that the more I put into it, the more meaningful I find the experience, so there is much to recommend doing this privately even if there is no wider dedication to work meditatively.

Rituals frequently include sharing of drink and food – cake and mead are most popular, but wine, bread, cider, beer, fruit juice, biscuits and other goodies all turn up too. Here again someone will speak to the group, asking that the food and drink be blessed, and offering the first of each to the earth. These words can guide your meditation. Food is then distributed with the words 'may you never hunger' and liquid with 'may you never thirst'. Accepting food and drink, and thoughtfully accepting this blessing, contemplate the nourishment you have been given. Think about where it came from, who made it, how it grew. Be aware of the sun and rain within it, and the skills it represents. Land, ancestry and community combine in the food we share. Be conscious of the energy you are taking into yourself. And enjoy the experience!

As the ritual unwinds, you will have the same set of opportunities to contemplate as you did on the way in. You may want to focus your attention in the same way, or take the opportunity to do something different.

At the end of the ritual, take a few moments to be still and quiet. You might want to walk the perimeters once again, conscious of the spirits of place. Take the time to offer your private farewells and thanks. During this post-ritual time, you will likely be in a different state of awareness to usual. You may feel more open and receptive. Don't rush to leave that space, but give yourself time to shift gently, just as you would when coming out of deep meditation. You may find this is a good time for inspiration.

Some circles lend themselves more to meditative approaches than others. How able you are to explore privately within a public context will depend on the character of the circle, and perhaps on your role within it. Some groups can be inherently quiet and reflective even when they are not overtly exploring meditations. Other groups are dynamic and chaotic in ways that could make meditation difficult. Highly scripted and structured working groups may not give you enough space to work your own meditation alongside the organized aspects.

If you are working with a grove or a closed ritual group, you may want to discuss the possibilities of bringing private meditation practice into group ritual. It could be very effective to share ritual whilst simultaneously exploring private meditation.

Contributing Meditation to Ritual

The structure of your ritual group will inform how viable it is for you to contribute meditation work to the mix. If you lead a group or are part of the core holding it, then you have the means to suggest adding meditation to ritual. In many groups you will undoubtedly find that even without being an organizer, you can offer to contribute a guided meditation to the ritual, and will have your offer welcomed. Some groups will not be open to this however. If a group works to pre-designed rituals, then you may find there is no scope for adding to the agreed form. Not everyone likes to meditate, so you may find it isn't what others want in their circle. If meditating in group ritual really speaks to you and you have no appropriate place in which to explore that, you may need to try and establish a group and draw likeminded people to you.

There are practical issues around leading meditations in a ritual context, and they need considering well before you start anything. In a large circle, precise, guided meditation based on a sharing of words, is difficult. I've been in circles of over a hundred at Avebury, when you have to shout to make words carry, there are non-participants watching, and new people joining the circle all the time. In such circumstances, organizing a detailed meditation like a pathworking is nigh on impossible. You might be able to encourage people to contemplate an idea, but detailed guidance will be too difficult. The size of the circle is a very important consideration, along with how well you can make your voice carry, and how able and willing you are to shout if needs be. With open rituals, the size of circle can be unpredictable. In the same Gorsedd, I've been in circles of a dozen, and circles of over forty. That potential for change in numbers can seriously affect meditation, and the not knowing in advance means you have to be able to flex according to what you get on the day. Even in closed groups, numbers can vary unexpectedly.

If you are working outside, then the weather has a huge influence on the way ritual happens. Again, you need to be able to flex according to what occurs on the day. Either pick meditations that are inherently flexible for numbers and conditions, have several in mind to choose between in response to what you get, or be able to improvise and change things at the last moment to suit the ritual.

Open Groups and Closed Group Issues

Closed groups have a fixed membership, where everyone knows everyone else, and outsiders are not usually welcome. People will only be able to attend with permission. Open groups are available to anyone who wants to come along on the day, so you can find family groups, people from other traditions, and even the odd policeman in your circle. Some groups run a halfway house arrangement; either offering a mix of open and closed rituals, or having a core group who are permitted to bring additional folk along. Every possibility here affects the potential makeup of the group, the degree of uncertainty you have over who will be there, and the intimacy of relationship between group members. These are all issues that affect how you meditate within the ritual.

As discussed in the section on meditation groups, meditating can create intensely personal and affecting experiences. In a closed ritual group or grove, where there is trust and people are used to each other, then this may be both appropriate and welcome. Closed groups create scope for discussing the meditation and sharing what is learned as well. There is possibility for deeper working, and for sharing the responsibility of leading the meditations. A closed group gives you much the same possibilities as a dedicated meditation group.

In open rituals, people attending may be strangers to each other, or they may have the kind of loose acquaintance that makes many people uncomfortable with openness. Meditations for open rituals need to be offered at an appropriate level, not demanding too much emotional exposure for participants. For open rituals, there is much to be said for focusing on physical meditations and simpler acts of communing. To invite a circle to connect with the land or the immediate surroundings is powerful, and unlikely to trouble anyone. You can invite people to contemplate a concept for a while, and share their experiences. Focusing on broad, relevant topics is best here. Good topics include our relationship with the current season, the land, service, environmental action, peace, justice, the elements, the ancestors, spirits of place, community, healing, creativity, myths, and recent news issues, for example. Working in this way can introduce a strong philosophical element to what is then shared in ritual – which brings its own benefits.

The Practicalities, Indoors, Outdoors
Most Druid groups I have encountered favor working outdoors. Some undoubtedly will work inside, especially in inclement weather, which is fairly easy from a meditation perspective. All of the issues discussed around indoors gatherings for meditation groups will apply here, but will be easier because you probably already have a space defined. Furthermore, the meditation leader is not necessarily responsible for creating the whole atmosphere in this context. In many ways, taking responsibility for inserting a meditation into the ritual of an indoor-working closed group, is about as easy as it gets for running guided meditations.

As previously discussed, working outside creates practical issues and these are just as pertinent for rituals as for meditation groups. Are you going to ask people to stand, or sit? Can they do that comfortably? A cold, damp bottom is an unpleasant distraction and most folks will not appreciate it! If you have a closed group who are known to you then warning them in advance can make meditating in ritual a lot easier as they will be practically prepared. However, open groups are unpredictable and you can't always get word out to everyone who might turn up. Open groups frequently attract families and children. Much as I love having children in ritual, most of them cannot handle quiet meditative situations. How will you deal with them? Can you include them? Can you find them something else to do? What about adults who aren't inclined to participate?

The weather has a huge impact on outdoors ritual and meditation. You can't predict it more than a few days in advance, and you certainly can't control it. I've been to numerous rituals in the open air when the conditions were challenging; windswept gatherings at Avebury where folk had to shout to make themselves heard across the circle, a mud-laden, rain-soaked Lugnasadh in the woods, Imbolc in a snowstorm and Samhain with added thunder. When the weather is challenging, long meditations are going to be difficult for most people. In such conditions, rituals are often abridged, and sometimes cancelled. People don't tend to linger when the rain is soaking through their coats and their feet are going numb. While an individual may choose to meditate in such conditions, these are not circumstances in which to attempt group ritual meditation – especially not of a quiet and stationary sort. Sometimes the only thing to do is admit defeat and ditch the meditation. If the setting isn't right, don't be afraid to acknowledge it and move on. Druidry is about listening to the land and the elements, if they are telling you to give up and go home, there's no shame in recognizing that, and very little to be gained from making people cold and miserable.

The best time of year for using pathworkings or visualizations in ritual is undoubtedly summer when there's a fighting chance people will be warm, comfortable and inclined to sit round. This assumes that you have the quiet necessary – other people in public spaces can disrupt this for you. And even in summer, thunderstorms, cold snaps, or an excess of heat can also throw your plans. Be prepared to change, improvise, or shorten what you had in mind, as conditions on the day require.

Meditations that contain a seasonal element tend to be popular and tie in well to the ritual. Whatever you choose to do, it's important to make the working relevant and accessible to those doing it. Therefore simple is often best. Meditation in ritual must contribute to the ritual in some way and make sense in the context of the whole – just throwing one in for the sake of it is unlikely to work. However, if the meditation is woven into the meaning and season of the ritual, it will likely enhance people's experiences, deepen the ritual and become a thing you can keep exploring. This means that if you are leading the meditation but not the ritual, you need to be planning in advance alongside whoever else is making preparations for the day. Some groups, through either confidence or inherent chaoticness, do not plan in advance to any great degree. This calls for an ability to respond on the day, improvising, reacting to the contributions of others, and going with the flow. It can work beautifully, and feel more integrated with the land, weather and people as you find them in the moment. I would recommend it as a way to start working. Planning builds confidence, experience builds the skills for improvisation. When you have confidence and experience to rely on, improvising becomes a lot easier, and even guided meditations can be made up in the spur of the moment.

If you are inserting a meditation into a ritual, then it should be placed in the main body of the ritual. There is much to be said for doing it shortly before any bardic expression in the plan, and before the bread and mead sharing. These activities are great for grounding people, and you will struggle to get a meditative atmosphere after them.

If you have a closed group then you have the freedom to explore how long and how deeply you want to meditate. With open groups, there is always the likelihood of a new face and you cannot assume people are all going to be familiar with what you are doing. For open groups, meditations need to be fairly simple and easy to get into. They should not be too long – quarter of an hour is going to be your upper limit for anything non-physical. As with other group meditations, you will need to pay close attention to how people are responding.

While you may be able to assume that everyone at the ritual is pagan, you can't assume that they all follow the same gods, or any gods for that matter. Animists, Dianics, Druids, Heathens, Wiccans, Pagan Atheists, and Druid Christians can all find themselves in the same circle, with all kinds of others, and perhaps a few folk who are new to all of this and still finding their way. You cannot assume that references will be recognized, symbols entirely shared or worldviews entirely correspond. Bear this in mind when planning your meditation. Try to keep the meditation as open as you can. If you want to take people into the imagery of a specific myth or the energies of a specific deity, don't spring it on them, talk first about what you want to do, give folk a chance to step back if it isn't for them, and make sure everyone goes in prepared, and comfortable.

Give people space to share their experiences afterwards as this will be helpful for them, and is a good intermittent stage between the meditating and the rest of the ritual. All the observations about managing this for groups apply equally here.

Meditations for Open Ritual Groups

When it comes to meditation in ritual, I favor methods that include an active element. As before suggested, having people contemplate a concept or season for a little while and feedback works well, but to go further without becoming inaccessible or weather-challenged, the physically based approaches work best, I find.

I've explored meditation in ritual over a number of years, although I am not sure that the people working with me were always consciously relating to the work as meditation. Part of the beauty of the suggestions below is that people can come into them at whatever level suits them. Someone deep in their Druidry and well experienced at meditating can work seriously with these scenarios. Those entirely new to it, with no idea of how to meditate, can potter along and get something good from the experience. And anything in between. It's viable to include children in this kind of activity – they won't disrupt it, or get bored. Most people who don't like to meditate can find ways of working with these, and you can have a couple of dozen people all at different levels, all working together in their own ways at the same time.

If you ask people to stand or sit in circle for a prolonged meditation, they can get restless and distract each other. Children rapidly become a liability, those who don't have the concentration or inclination feel awkward. If you are working outside, there are a great many possibilities that come from breaking the circle and sending people out on their own for ten minutes or so. Anyone can do these, it all works with children, and people seldom disturb each other. You will find some people not really working in a spiritual way, but instead using the time to chat and catch up with each other. That is their choice and don't be thrown or frustrated by it. By encouraging people out into nature, you are helping them find their own ways, even if they aren't doing what you wanted them to do. Some of them will respond to this. Even if they appear not to, the time spent outside is good for the soul. They might have things they need to express to someone, or they might not yet feel ready for more involved work. Given time and patience, this may change. So long as they are not preventing others from working, there is no problem with non-participation. If no one seems to be going with the meditation, then you have issues and may need a re-think. Talk to people and find out what's going on, don't judge, and take it as an opportunity to learn.

Send people out of the circle to contemplate the season and see how it is showing itself in the world around them. Give them ten to fifteen minutes and then call them back to share observations.

If you are working at night with a fire or lanterns, invite people to step into the darkness for a while and experience it, then return and share their impressions.

Invite people to walk the perimeter of the space you use and contemplate the nature of the space, and then share.

If you have plenty of trees in your ritual space, invite people to go and stand with the trees, briefly describe to them how to connect with the tree, to imagine themselves as rooted in the soil, to listen to the tree and just to be with it. If you have other environmental features, such as rocks, water and birds, then you can explore these in the same ways.

Invite people to imagine the ancestors who lived, worked or travelled this land. Send them out to walk as their ancestors and invite them to come back with whatever ideas occur to them.

Send people out to find an object that speaks to them and invite them to get to know it, listen to its voice, and bring it back to share with the others.

Invite people to collect natural objects from the area and bring them back to make an improvised mandala or altar space.

Encourage people to use charcoal, mud or other natural resources to create some private image or expression as an offering to the land, or a collective image even, if space permits. Do not leave anything permanent without permission as this may attract the wrong sort of attention.

Invite people to seek out a small, natural item they can take away with them as a focus for their own private ritual. Do not take anything living.

Encourage people to listen to the space you are using, to the natural sounds, the evidence of human presence and the voice of spirit.

All of these exercises, and any others you can invent in the same vein, fit well into open rituals. People can approach them in any way they like. It's easy to get the hang of and anyone can do it. Children will take the opportunity to run around and play, which is not usually disruptive of this kind of work. People who need to go deeper will simply take themselves off further to find the necessary quiet. You may have fun rounding them up again. Bards in your circle may choose to stay at the center and provide gentle music – which can be very effective. If you make yourself available to people who have questions or need support, that can help the less confident in your circle get to grips with the experience.

As with all other forms of meditation, the chance to feed back and be heard without judgment is very important. Make sure everyone has opportunity to speak. However, in the context of a Druid ritual, this element of the process can acquire new and interesting dimensions. Where there are bards, there is creativity. You may find people returning with fragments of poetry, songs they have remembered, tunes inspired by the trees, stories recalled from families or histories. Given time and space, this kind of wild and unstructured meditating can be a tremendous source of inspiration, and you may find you roll very naturally from the meditation into the bardic celebration in your ritual.

Implications of Meditation for Magical Practice

For a number of working groups, magic is very much the point of ritual. I think this is truer of Wiccan groups than Druidic ones, but there are plenty of folk who blend the two or work eclecti-cally and there are Druid groups exploring magical practice. Again, this is too vast a subject to cover within this book, so I shall simply focus on the ways in which meditation is involved in the process.

By 'magic' I do not necessarily mean the kind of spells associated with fantasy fiction. Magic is change and transfor-mation, whether we seek that within ourselves or in the wider world. It is the focusing of will to bring intention into reality. Every action begins with intention. Life is a consequence of will, so the making manifest of will is not necessarily a 'supernatural' activity. However, without clarity and focus, establishing will and intent is hard, even for entirely non-magical activities. Meditation gives us tools for analysis, insight and clarity. It can also enable us to focus attention. A lone individual can focus their intent by any method that suits them. Group ritual magic requires group focus, and again, meditation can play a part here. If your understanding of magic is about spells and is more witch-craft-derived, then using meditation to focus your intent works very well. Equally, if magic means self-transformation, inspiration, and something a touch less 'occult' meditation is still a great enabler.

I am neither a magical practitioner nor a Wiccan, but my reading has taken me in all kinds of directions and I have explored a little for myself. What I have read of magical practice, especially for groups, calls for shared visualization. This is essentially a meditation skill given extra magical oomph. You might be visualizing a cone of power, the magical circle in which your group works, or an outcome you are seeking. Whatever the requirement, the ability to visualize is a critically important one. Groups who wish to explore ritual magic will very likely benefit from exploring ritual meditation together first. Visualization is a skill, and one that benefits from practice. The more time you devote to visualizing a thing, the easier it is to picture. Following from this, the more time you spend visualizing, the easier it is to see how to bring intention to fruition. Sometimes just believing a thing is possible, is half of the fight.

If we can imagine something, we have a greater chance of making it so. Whether or not you believe in magic in any way, it is certainly true that action begins with intent. The better developed the intention, the clearer and better focused it is, the better your chances. When it comes to the magic of transforming yourself and changing your inner life, the ability to imagine and visualize the change is powerful indeed. We can recreate and rediscover ourselves through ritual, magic and meditation. If we can imagine ourselves differently, we have already begun moving towards the change. If we can hold the idea of doing, or achieving something, that will help us find the necessary confidence to see it through. Is that magic? I think so. By pouring creative energy into positive thought forms and powerful intentions, we build our sense of the world and our place within it, and from there we can progress into doing. A person who does not believe in change, will struggle to change.

For me, ritual is magic, there doesn't need to be any predetermined intention to make that happen. Simply gathering, sharing, and experiencing in a mindful way creates change within those present. That magic will find its own ways on into the world. It is possible to do more than that, acting in a deliberate way. In sharing our intent we make each other stronger, help each other to stay true to our aims, reinforce the idea that we can affect change, and bring the desired change closer.

Earlier, I talked about the relationship between meditation and shamanism, and the difficulty of determining the point at which meditation becomes trance. There's also a very fine line between magic and psychological process. When the change begins within us, how much of that do we ascribe to the effect of changing our thought forms, and how much to magic? If we become stronger, braver, clearer of intent, that can feel incredibly magical. I'm not convinced it's even useful in this context to be seeking a clear dividing line between magic and psychology. If the language of magic inspires and enables you to make change, then use and celebrate it. And equally, if the language of rationality, psychology and self-help gives you a firmer footing, use that instead. Talk about self-empowerment, or talk about magical transformation, or both. Embrace what works, and enjoy your own understanding of the world. We are never going to have fixed right answers about these things, so we may as well go with what moves us.

Those who talk about our culture, our world, sustainability and solutions are increasingly saying that we can't look for the change to come from outside. All the resources we have to build a better world lie within us, and reside in the land. There is nothing else. To make change, we must first change ourselves. No matter what it is we seek, we will have to look inward if we are to find it, as well as questing in external reality. The process of change is one in which we are always included, we cannot be separate from it. Whatever magic and transformation we seek, meditation gives skills that will help us on our way – self-awareness, the ability to stop and think, the habit of deep contemplation.

Conclusions

When it comes to practicing Druidry, meditation is one tool among many. I find it a very good and useful way of working, one that underpins much of what I do. Meditation is not Druidry however, although you can structure a Druidic life and practice that is very meditation-centric. To be a Druid is to take Druidic principles and ways of being into every aspect of your life. There are times and places where meditation cannot go, but Druidry must. The skills of meditation – the discipline, self-control, self-awareness and capacity for deep contemplation are vastly useful for anyone seeking a thoughtful, self-possessed existence – Druidic or otherwise.

Meditation is no substitute for living and doing in the 'real' world – unless you find yourself unable to participate in that for some reason. For anyone limited in their ability to get out and participate, meditation can be a helpful way of learning, experiencing and exploring. Meditation should be part of living, experiencing and acting, not separate from it. Like anything else in this life, taken to excess it can be damaging. If meditation is taking you away from experience and relationship, then you are doing too much, or doing it in an unproductive way. To meditate well and effectively as a Druid is to commune more deeply with the rest of existence.

Sometimes the meditative journeys will bring insights or awareness we cannot rationally explain. Sometimes it may feel more 'real' than our regular lives. Holding onto a sense of where consensus reality is and how other people perceive and engage is vital. This does not mean discounting or devaluing that 'other' knowing, it just calls for maintaining clarity about the differences. The work of Druidry is rooted in connection, and that means existing in relationship to others. However deeply we delve into our own minds, however far we travel in the realms of spirit, we must also be part of this world and present within it to function as people. To lose track of the differences between inner and outer realities is to court madness and serves nothing. At the same time, there is little point in exploring through meditation only to reject anything out of the ordinary we find there. Balance is everything.

To be a Druid is to balance between thinking and doing, culture and nature, light and dark. It is the art of knowing the different worlds and ways of being, and walking between them. So too must we balance the inner life and the outer life, the things we know intuitively and that which we learn rationally.

Moon Books invites you to begin or deepen your encounter with Paganism, in all its rich, creative, flourishing forms.